TIMELESS RECIPES

THE HOME SHOPPING NETWORK

TIMELESS
RECIPES

Timeless Recipes

This cookbook is a collection of favorite recipes,
which are not necessarily original recipes.

TIMELESS RECIPES

Library of Congress Catalog Number: 98-075166
ISBN: 0-9667024-0-9

Edited, Designed, and Manufactured by Favorite Recipes® Press
an imprint of

P.O. Box 305142, Nashville, Tennessee 37230
1-800-358-0560

Manufactured in the United States of America

First Printing: 1998   50,000 copies

Timeless Recipes

Table of Contents

Preface – 6

Dedication – 7

Thank You – 7

Off Camera – 8

Candid Kitchens –126

Index – 173

Timeless Recipes

Preface

Family is the heart of America. Family means our home, our traditions, our cultures. It's our past, present, and future. It's the glue that holds our country together.

Many of our show hosts say they feel like they have two families: the folks at home and the people they come in contact with everyday through The Home Shopping Network. This unique cookbook brings these families together. In this special book, our hosts share very personal parts of their lives. They tell about treasured family recipes handed down through generations. They share personal anecdotes. Among the many recipe offerings are ethnic delights that reflect proud heritages, elegant gourmet ideas, and home-style country cooking. Quite simply, it's good cooking...brought to you by your favorite TV show hosts from The Home Shopping Network.

No matter what the country or culture of origin, family also means food—good food shared with the people you care about.

The recipes in this book have been compiled with love, best wishes, and, yes, even a few tears as the hosts searched their memories and family archives for recipes special enough to share with you.

Timeless Recipes

Dedication

The Home Shopping Network fondly dedicates
this book to Steve Chaney,
a man who is known and loved literally
around the world.

Thank You

We want to thank the hosts who have given of their time and talents to help create this cookbook for you. To ensure that the book is most helpful to you, we've had each recipe tested by nutrition and cooking experts. But, most importantly, these recipes have been tested by time...and have become our family favorites. We hope they will become your family favorites, too.

Our hosts all want you to know that we had so much fun putting this book together. Now, we are proud to pass it on to you. Savor these recipes with your family and friends, or make something special just for yourself. We hope you have fun using this cookbook. Please let us know how you like it. Bon appetit!

OFF CAMERA

From Our Homes to Yours

Yours

Liz Benbrook was an on air model at The Home Shopping Network before becoming a show host in 1994. She attended Monmouth College in Illinois. Liz has professional experience in sales, theatre and education. She wanted to become a show host because, she says, "It seemed a natural blend of my sales and on-camera experience." Liz says the most important part about being a show host is: "The people...I know we perform a real service for many people."

Country Onion Tart

2 pounds onions, thinly
  sliced
¼ cup water
3 tablespoons olive oil
1 teaspoon salt
2 eggs, lightly beaten

1 tablespoon Dijon mustard
1 baked (10-inch) tart shell
5 oil-packed anchovy fillets,
  patted dry, julienned
12 to 15 niçoise or geata olives

Combine the onions, water, olive oil and salt in a 6-quart Dutch oven. Braise, covered, for 30 minutes, stirring occasionally; drain. Let stand until cool. Stir in the eggs.

Spread the Dijon mustard over the bottom of the tart shell. Top with the onion mixture. Create a lattice pattern with the anchovy strips over the onion mixture. Arrange an olive in each diamond.

Place the tart on the middle oven rack. Bake at 425 degrees for 30 to 40 minutes or until golden brown.

Yields 8 servings

LIZ BENBROOK

My earliest and most

treasured memories are set in

my grandmother's kitchen.

They play in my mind in a

continuous and unending

haze of laughter and of loving.

Christmas Cake

¹/₂ cup finely chopped pecans	4 eggs
8 ounces cream cheese, softened	2¹/₄ cups sifted cake flour
1 cup butter or margarine, softened	1¹/₂ teaspoons baking powder
1¹/₂ cups sugar	1 (6-ounce) jar maraschino cherries, drained, chopped
1¹/₂ teaspoons vanilla extract	¹/₂ cup chopped pecans
1¹/₂ teaspoons cinnamon	1¹/₂ cups sifted confectioners' sugar
¹/₄ teaspoon nutmeg	2 tablespoons milk
	food coloring (optional)

Grease a 10-inch bundt pan. Sprinkle with ¹/₂ cup pecans.

Combine the cream cheese, butter, sugar, vanilla, cinnamon and nutmeg in a mixer bowl. Beat until blended, scraping the bowl occasionally. Add the eggs 1 at a time, beating well after each addition. Sift 2 cups of the cake flour and baking powder together. Add to the batter and mix well.

Combine the remaining ¹/₄ cup cake flour, cherries and ¹/₂ cup pecans in a bowl. Fold into the batter. Spoon into the prepared pan. Bake at 325 degrees for 1 to 1¹/₄ hours or until the cake tests done. Cool in the pan for 5 minutes. Remove to a wire rack to cool completely.

Combine the confectioners' sugar and milk in a bowl, stirring until of a glaze consistency. Add food coloring and mix well. Drizzle over the cake. Garnish with pecan halves, cherries, crushed peppermint candy and/or candy sprinkles.

Yield: 16 servings

The taste of delicious food is somehow interwoven with the taste of the companionship in my grandmother's kitchen, and the scent of bread baking or a turkey roasting is the symbol of the sense of belonging that I felt. Food and family—sustenance for body and soul.

Through the years, the group in my grandmother's kitchen grew larger. Teenaged sons, my uncles, came to "help" but mostly to raid. I learned to make the mashed potatoes sitting on an uncle's knee. It was a large and youthful hand that covered my small one on the old-fashioned potato masher. To this day, I leave some lumps in my mashed potatoes, because that young man of long ago liked lumps in the mashed potatoes.

Today, another young man (my 16-year-old son) helps to make the mashed potatoes in my very own kitchen. He fusses about the lumps, but he leaves a few for me, because he knows that somehow they are important. Just as my sons bring girlfriends who become wives, so also did my uncles bring home the young women who are my aunts. The measure of whether we really want to keep them has a lot to do with whether or not they help set the table! And just as I learned to cook at my grandmother's table, so also has my daughter learned from her grandmothers and from me.

My mom, my sister Sandra, and my aunt Elaine all went to a cooking school in the south of France, and those of us who didn't go along have vicariously enjoyed the experience again and again at the family table.

Stove-Top Eye-of-Round with Spring Vegetables

1 (2-pound) eye-of-round roast
½ teaspoon coarsely ground pepper
2 teaspoons vegetable oil
2 beef bouillon cubes
1 clove of garlic, cut into halves
2½ cups water
1 bay leaf
½ teaspoon dried tarragon
1¼ pounds baby carrots, trimmed
1¾ pounds small white and/or red potatoes
1½ pounds thin asparagus, trimmed, cooked

Pat the roast dry with paper towels; rub with the pepper. Brown the roast on all sides in the oil in a 5-quart Dutch oven over medium-high heat. Insert a meat thermometer into the thickest portion of the roast. Add the bouillon cubes, garlic, water, bay leaf and tarragon. Bring to a boil and reduce the heat. Simmer, covered, for 20 minutes.

Add the carrots and potatoes. Bring to a boil and reduce the heat. Simmer, covered, for 30 minutes or until the vegetables are tender and the meat thermometer registers 140 degrees.

Remove the roast to a warm platter. Internal temperature will rise to 145 degrees. Remove the carrots and potatoes to the platter with a slotted spoon, reserving the cooking liquid in the Dutch oven. Add the asparagus to the platter. Discard the garlic and bay leaf. Skim the cooking liquid. Serve with the roast and vegetables.

Yields 8 servings

TINA BERRY

Cajun Red Beans and Rice

1 cup finely chopped onions
1 cup finely chopped green
   bell peppers
1 large clove of garlic,
   minced
1 (15-ounce) can dark red
   kidney beans, rinsed,
   drained

1 (14-ounce) can low-sodium
   low-fat chicken broth
1 cup long-grain white rice
2 ounces fat-free smoked ham or
   turkey breast, finely chopped
1 bay leaf
½ teaspoon dried thyme
salt to taste

Combine the onions, green peppers and garlic in a large
nonstick saucepan. Cook over medium heat for 3 minutes, stirring
frequently. Add the beans, broth, rice, ham, bay leaf, thyme
and salt and mix well. Bring to a boil. Simmer, covered, for
20 minutes or until the rice is tender and the liquid is absorbed.
Fluff the mixture with a fork. Discard the bay leaf.

   Yields 4 servings

Poached Salmon Steaks

1 cup white wine

¼ cup fresh lemon or lime
    juice

2 teaspoons Dijon mustard

½ cup finely chopped onion
    or shallots

4 (4-ounce) salmon steaks, less
    than 1 inch thick

2 teaspoons capers

1½ tablespoons cornstarch
    (optional)

¼ cup cold water

Combine the wine, lemon juice, mustard and onion in a large
nonstick skillet and mix well. Bring to a boil. Simmer for
10 minutes or until reduced. Add the salmon. Simmer, covered,
for 9 minutes or until opaque, turning once. Stir in the capers.
Whisk the cornstarch and ¼ cup of cold water together in a
small bowl. Pour into the skillet. Cook until sauce is of the desired
consistency, stirring constantly.

Yields 4 servings

Mango-Basil Salsa

2 ripe mangoes, peeled,
    pitted, chopped

½ red bell pepper, chopped,
    seeds reserved

½ cup fresh orange juice

juice of 2 limes

¼ cup finely chopped basil

salt (optional)

freshly ground pepper

Combine the mangoes, red bell pepper, orange juice, lime juice,
basil, salt and pepper in a medium bowl and mix well. Chill,
covered, for 2 hours or longer.

Yields 2 cups

Italian Cream Cake

½ cup butter or margarine, softened

½ cup shortening

2 cups sugar

5 egg yolks

1 tablespoon vanilla extract

2 cups flour

1 teaspoon baking soda

1 cup buttermilk

1 cup flaked coconut

5 egg whites

Nutty Cream Cheese Frosting (see page 20)

Cream the butter and shortening in a mixer bowl at medium speed until fluffy. Add the sugar gradually, beating until light. Beat in the egg yolks 1 at a time. Mix in the vanilla.

Mix the flour and baking soda together. Add to the creamed mixture alternately with the buttermilk, mixing well at low speed after each addition and beginning and ending with the flour mixture. Stir in the coconut.

Beat the egg whites in a mixer bowl until stiff peaks form. Fold gently into the batter. Spoon into 3 greased and floured 9-inch cake pans.

Bake at 350 degrees for 25 minutes or until a wooden pick inserted into the center comes out clean. Cool in the pans on wire racks for 10 minutes. Remove to wire racks to cool completely.

Spread Nutty Cream Cheese Frosting between the layers and over the top and side of the cake.

Yields 12 servings

BOBBI RAY CARTER

One of the most enjoyable experiences that I have with my daughter Noelle is in the kitchen. But unlike traditional cooking, we love to be creative. I love when it is raining outside. We spend the day playing games and "creating" fun foods in the kitchen.

Nutty Cream Cheese Frosting

1 cup chopped pecans
8 ounces cream cheese, softened
½ cup butter or margarine, softened

1 tablespoon vanilla extract
1 (16-ounce) package confectioners' sugar, sifted

Spread the pecans in a shallow baking pan. Bake at 350 degrees for 5 to 10 minutes or until toasted, stirring occasionally. Let cool.

Beat the cream cheese, butter and vanilla at medium speed in a mixer bowl until light. Beat in the confectioners' sugar at low speed until blended. Beat at high speed until smooth. Stir in the pecans.

Bobbi and Noelle's Designer Fluffer Nutter

peanut butter to taste
2 slices bread
pancake syrup to taste

marshmallow fluff to taste
cinnamon to taste

Spread the peanut butter on one slice of bread. Swirl the syrup in a curlicue over the peanut butter. Spread the marshmallow fluff on the other slice of bread. Sprinkle the cinnamon over the fluff. Invert onto the peanut butter to form a sandwich.

Yields 1 serving

Bobbi Ray Carter

Sweet Potato Crunch

4 large sweet potatoes,
   cooked, mashed

3 eggs

1 cup sugar

$\frac{1}{2}$ cup milk

1 cup melted margarine

2 teaspoons vanilla extract

1 cup packed brown sugar

$\frac{1}{2}$ cup flour

1 cup chopped pecans

Combine the sweet potatoes, eggs, sugar, milk, $\frac{1}{2}$ cup of the melted margarine and vanilla in a bowl and mix well. Pour into a greased 2-quart baking dish. Combine the brown sugar, flour, pecans and the remaining melted margarine in a separate bowl and mix well. Sprinkle on top of the sweet potato mixture. Bake at 350 degrees for 1 hour.

    Yields 6 to 8 servings

Buckeyes

1$\frac{1}{2}$ cups peanut butter

3 cups sugar

1 cup margarine, softened

1 teaspoon vanilla extract

3 (12-ounce) packages
   semisweet chocolate chips

Combine the peanut butter, sugar, margarine and vanilla in a bowl and mix well. Roll into small balls. Chill for 2 or more hours. Melt the chocolate chips over low heat in a saucepan, stirring constantly. Dip the balls $\frac{3}{4}$ of the way into the chocolate and place on waxed paper. Let stand until cool. Store in an airtight container in the refrigerator.

    Yields 84 buckeyes

Noelle and I have come up with some pretty interesting combinations of "kid-friendly" foods that are also an ageless love for adults!

Our recipe for Fluffer Nutter was a result of many different trials with all kinds of crazy ingredients—both Noelle and I love it and hope you will too!

Janie came to The Home

Shopping Network in 1997

from a background in theater.

She says, "I have produced,

directed, costumed, and

performed in musical theater

for the past 18 years."

After closing her theater in

Vermont, she wanted to stay

in entertainment and so went

to an audition for The Home

Shopping Network. Janie

says the most important

thing about being a show

host is "the comfort, joy,

and entertainment we bring

to our viewers."

Daddy's Favorite Lemon Meringue Pie

My dad has a wicked sweet tooth, so when his sweet tooth is aching, he will just go into the kitchen and whip himself up a Lemon Meringue Pie, one of our family's favorites.

1 (14-ounce) can sweetened condensed milk	1 (8-inch) graham cracker pie shell
2 large egg yolks	2 large egg whites
½ cup fresh lemon juice	¼ teaspoon cream of tartar
grated peel of 1 lemon	2 tablespoons sugar

Combine the sweetened condensed milk, egg yolks, lemon juice and lemon peel in a mixer bowl and beat until the mixture thickens. Pour into the pie shell.

Beat the egg whites and cream of tartar in a mixer bowl until stiff peaks form. Beat in the sugar gradually. Spread over the pie, sealing to the edge.

Bake at 350 degrees for 5 minutes or just until the meringue is golden brown. Chill until serving time.

Yields 6 servings

JANIE CHARNOW

Grandmother Childs' Sugar Tea Cakes

Going to Grandmother Childs' house meant you would always be able to choose from numerous desserts every evening: Caramel Cake, Fried Apple Tarts, Coconut Cake, Chocolate Pound Cake, and many, many more. One of my all-time favorites was her Sugar Tea Cakes and that's the one I'd like to share with you.

1 cup margarine, softened	4½ cups flour
1 cup vegetable oil	1 teaspoon baking soda
1 cup sugar	1 teaspoon baking powder
2 eggs	1 teaspoon cream of tartar
2 teaspoons vanilla extract	1 cup confectioners' sugar

Cream the margarine and oil in a bowl. Add the sugar, eggs and vanilla and mix well. Sift the flour, baking soda, baking powder, cream of tartar and confectioners' sugar together. Add to the creamed mixture and mix well. Drop by ½ teaspoonfuls onto greased cookie sheets. Bake at 350 degrees for 12 to 15 minutes or until light brown. Cool on wire racks.

Yields 100 tea cakes

"...an amazing woman, my Grandmother Childs."

My Grandmother Childs had a little bakery where she created the most beautiful wedding cakes. She made wedding cakes for her six children, her 24 grandchildren, and other clients, one being the nephew of President Eisenhower— an amazing woman, my Grandmother Childs.

Janie Charnow

Mom's Corn Bread Dressing

Another great cook is my mom, Jane Childs Hostetter. Mom would put together a wonderful feast every Sunday and all holidays. As I grew older, one of my favorite dishes became Mom's Corn Bread Dressing. Put this with a fresh juicy turkey and you're in heaven.

2 cups chopped onions	1 teaspoon celery seed
butter or margarine	1 teaspoon sage
3 cups chopped celery	1 teaspoon salt
2 to 3 cups broth	2 tablespoons poultry
6 cups crumbled corn bread	seasoning
3 cups crumbled day-old or	3 eggs, beaten
toasted white bread	

Sauté onions in a small amount of butter in a skillet until tender; do not brown. Sauté celery in a small amount of butter in a skillet until tender; do not brown. Heat the broth in a small saucepan. Combine the corn bread, white bread, celery seeds, sage, salt, poultry seasoning, eggs, sautéed onions and celery in a large bowl. Add enough broth to moisten and mix well. Place mixture in a greased 6x13-inch baking pan. Bake at 350 degrees for 40 minutes or until browned. Serve with Giblet Gravy (page 157).

Yields 15 to 16 servings

I grew up making all the southern dishes and making my own modifications. Since I married into a Jewish family, my horizons have expanded, and I have fallen in love with such wonderful dishes as Knaelach, Passover Bagels, Matzo Brie, Matzo Ball Soup, and my very favorite—Kasha Varniskes. I learned a lot from Grandma Tilly (my father-in-law's mother).

A native of St. Petersburg, Florida, Alice Cleveland attended St. Petersburg Junior College and Lee College in Baytown, Texas. Before becoming a show host in 1985, Alice worked in real estate sales as a motivational speaker and as a regional sales rep for the Associated Airlines School. She says she wanted to a be a show host because "I enjoy people, and I loved the interaction the host had with the viewers...plus I like to talk, I love sales, and I enjoy shopping—a natural combination for any woman!"

Vietnamese Chicken Salad

2 cups chopped cooked chicken
1 head cabbage, shredded
1 onion, finely chopped
½ cup sliced almonds
½ cup vegetable oil
⅓ cup apple cider vinegar
juice of 2 limes
2 packets artificial sweetener
salt and pepper to taste

Combine the chicken, cabbage, onion and almonds in a bowl and mix gently.

Blend the oil, vinegar, lime juice and artificial sweetener in a small bowl. Add to the chicken mixture and toss to coat well. Season with salt and pepper. Serve immediately or chill until serving time.

May substitute commercial Italian salad dressing or oil and vinegar for the dressing recipe. May add 1 chopped red or green bell pepper.

Yields 6 to 8 servings

ALICE CLEVELAND

I hope this wonderful

tummy-filling dish will be

enjoyed by others as much as

we've enjoyed making and

eating this for years. Not

only is it a delicous dessert,

but it makes a great

breakfast as well.

Growing up in the hills of Kentucky provided a beautiful surrounding, but it was a very repressed coal mining and logging town. We were very poor, like most of our neighbors in the tiny community in eastern Kentucky. It was not unusual for us to get our water from the well and bathe in a galvanized washtub. I've made the statement: "The biggest advantage I had was growing up disadvantaged." We learned early in life to appreciate everything, whether it was a hand-me-down dress or a yummy dessert made from stale bread and fresh cow's milk.

The recipe for my Grandmother's Bread Pudding is especially dear to me because of those early childhood days. I can remember my mom freezing the old bread and biscuits until she had enough to make a batch of the pudding. Daddy would milk our one and only milk cow and bring the still-warm milk in to Mom to use in the pudding. My sisters and I would watch Mom mix the simple ingredients of this anxiously awaited treat. Many times we would have it with a glass of warm milk before retiring to bed. By the way, I abhor warm milk today! But it is amazing what you'll drink when you don't know any better. (chuckle...) What I loved then and still do today is the sweet moist pudding made with those few simple ingredients and lots of love! This is a recipe and story that will always be passed down in our family.

Alice Cleveland

Bread Pudding

8 to 12 slices day-old bread, crumbled

1 to 1½ cups milk, scalded

¼ cup melted butter

1 to 1½ cups sugar

1 to 1½ teaspoons cinnamon

1 to 1½ teaspoons nutmeg

2 tablespoons vanilla extract

2 eggs

raisins (optional)

cinnamon-sugar to taste

Combine the bread, milk, butter, sugar, cinnamon, nutmeg, vanilla, eggs and raisins in a large bowl and mix well; bread should be completely saturated. Pour into a greased 9x13-inch baking dish. Sprinkle with cinnamon-sugar. Bake at 350 degrees for 45 to 60 minutes or until bread pudding is set. Serve with a favorite sauce.

Yields 15 servings

I sometimes wonder if it is the bread pudding I love so much or those memories of watching my grandmother and then my mom prepare this for us. Maybe it is actually a combination of the two.

"I hope this wonderful tummy-filling dish will be enjoyed by others..."

With a Bachelor of Arts

degree and a Master's in

Business Administration,

Brian Collard has a good

foundation in business.

Brian indulged his love of

sports by working as a

sportscaster before coming to

The Home Shopping

Network in 1986. One of

the aspects of his job that he

loves is the challenge of

spending three hours a day

on live television.

Tacos

1 pound ground beef	shredded lettuce
1 envelope taco seasoning mix	1 small onion, sliced
	shredded cheese
large taco shells	sour cream
2 tomatoes, sliced	taco sauce

Brown the ground beef in a skillet, stirring until crumbly; drain. Add the seasoning mix and prepare according to the package directions.

Spoon the ground beef mixture into the taco shells. Top with the tomatoes, lettuce, onion, cheese, sour cream and taco sauce.

Yields 4 servings

BRIAN COLLARD

Sloppy Joes

3 pounds ground beef
1 (15-ounce) can tomato
   sauce
$\frac{1}{2}$ cup catsup

$\frac{1}{4}$ cup packed brown sugar
2 tablespoons mustard
$\frac{1}{4}$ teaspoon vinegar
$\frac{1}{4}$ cup syrup

Cook the ground beef in a skillet, stirring until brown and crumbly; drain. Add the tomato sauce. Cover the top with catsup. Add the brown sugar, mustard, vinegar and syrup and mix well. Simmer for 2 hours, stirring occasionally.

Yields 12 servings

Chicken Enchiladas

1 (8-ounce) jar Cheez Whiz
2 cups shredded cooked
   chicken
$\frac{1}{3}$ cup ranch salad dressing

1 teaspoon chili powder
6 flour tortillas
$\frac{1}{2}$ cup salsa

Combine $\frac{1}{3}$ cup of the Cheez Whiz, chicken, ranch salad dressing and chili powder in a bowl and mix well. Spoon $\frac{1}{6}$ of mixture onto each tortilla. Roll up tortillas to enclose the filling. Place seam side down in a baking dish. Top with $\frac{1}{2}$ cup salsa. Bake at 350 degrees for 25 to 30 minutes. Place the remaining Cheez Whiz in a saucepan. Cook until melted, stirring constantly. Pour over the enchiladas.

Yields 6 servings

Brian Cottard

Meatballs and Spaghetti Sauce

5 (8-ounce) cans tomato sauce

4 (6-ounce) cans tomato paste

⅛ teaspoon sugar

salt and pepper to taste

garlic powder to taste

onion powder to taste

9 cups water

3 pounds lean ground beef

6 eggs, beaten

2¼ cups bread crumbs

chopped crushed parsley
to taste

Combine the tomato sauce, tomato paste, sugar, salt, pepper, garlic powder, onion powder and 9 cups water in a large stockpot and mix well. Combine the ground beef, eggs, bread crumbs, garlic powder, salt, pepper, onion powder and parsley in a large bowl and mix well. Shape into 1-inch balls. Brown on all sides in a skillet; drain. Add the meatballs to the sauce. Cook over medium heat for 3 hours or until the meatballs are cooked through.

Yields 30 to 40 meatballs

Connie is one of The Home Shopping Network's newest show hosts, having joined us only five months ago. She has a Bachelor's degree in Communications from the University of Tennessee. Before joining us, Connie worked at another shopping network for five years and also did feature sports reporting for television and radio. Hosting on The Home Shopping Network is the perfect enhancement for her two favorite hobbies— talking and shopping.

Sausage Heros with Peppers and Onions

1 pound sweet Italian sausage

$\frac{1}{4}$ cup water

2 medium red onions

1 red bell pepper

1 green bell pepper

$\frac{1}{3}$ cup water

4 (6-inch) hero rolls, split horizontally

Pierce the sausages all over with a fork. Combine with $\frac{1}{4}$ cup water in a 10-inch skillet and bring to a boil. Reduce the heat to low and cover. Simmer for 5 minutes. Remove the cover and increase the heat to medium. Cook until the sausages are brown and cooked through, turning occasionally. Drain on paper towels. Drain drippings, reserving 1 tablespoon in the skillet.

Cut the onions into halves lengthwise, then slice $\frac{1}{2}$ inch thick. Cut the bell peppers into $\frac{1}{2}$-inch strips. Add the onions and bell peppers to the reserved drippings in the skillet. Sauté for 15 minutes or until tender.

Slice the sausage into $\frac{1}{2}$-inch pieces. Add to the skillet with $\frac{1}{3}$ cup water, stirring to deglaze the skillet. Spoon the sausage mixture into the rolls.

Yields 4 servings

CONNIE CRAIG

Baked Fried Chicken

6 to 8 slices toasted bread

¹/₂ cup loosely packed
    parsley leaves

2 tablespoons grated nonfat
    Parmesan cheese

¹/₂ teaspoon thyme

¹/₂ teaspoon marjoram

¹/₂ teaspoon salt (optional)

¹/₄ teaspoon freshly ground
    pepper

2 egg whites

¹/₄ cup nonfat milk

1 large clove of garlic, minced

1 (2¹/₂-pound) chicken, skinned,
    defatted, cut up, wing tips
    and tail removed

Line a 9x13-inch baking pan with foil. Process the bread slices in a food processor until crumbly. Pour the bread crumbs into a shallow dish. Mince the parsley in the food processor, pulsing 4 or 5 times. Add the parsley, Parmesan cheese, thyme, marjoram, salt and pepper to the bread crumbs and mix well. Whisk the egg whites, milk and garlic in a shallow bowl until frothy. Dip the chicken into the egg mixture. Roll the chicken in the bread crumb mixture, coating well. Arrange the chicken in the prepared pan. Bake at 350 degrees for 35 to 45 minutes or until cooked through.

Yields 6 servings

Although I am certainly not a cook, I love nothing better than eating a good southern home-cooked meal. And being from East Tennessee, I've had lots of opportunities to eat great southern food.

Connie Craig

When I was very young, almost every Sunday my daddy and I would go to my mamaw's house to eat Sunday dinner. My grandmother was a great cook, and because she had eight children and was never quite sure who would be showing up for dinner, she would cook everything imaginable. On a typical Sunday, she would cook at least three or four different types of entrées (always including fried chicken), homemade rolls and biscuits, and various vegetables. Unfortunately, like some children, I was extremely finicky and, even in the face of all this wonderful food, all I wanted was a hot dog. I would ask my mamaw, and even after preparing all this food, she would fix me a hot dog. Needless to say, my tastes have changed a lot since then. Now there is nothing that can compete with fried chicken, creamed potatoes, and homemade biscuits (certainly not hot dogs). And I just wish I was half the cook that my mamaw was.

"...I love nothing better than eating a good southern home-cooked meal..."

Specializing in the late night shift, John Cremeans has been a show host for The Home Shopping Network since 1990. He worked in radio while still in high school, then went on to TV retailing at American Value Network and Cable Value Network. John says what is most important to him about being a show host at The Home Shopping Network is "the communication between me and the viewer. I really enjoy the fact that we provide a wonderful service to so many people."

Cremeans' Fettuccini Alfredo

My Alfredo recipe is a combination of different types of sauces that I have tried over the years. It is extremely rich and tends to change in flavor every time I use it. I've included a few variations of the Cremeans family favorite...see which one you like better.

8 ounces cream cheese, sliced
½ cup heavy cream
½ cup butter
1 cup grated Parmesan cheese

1 teaspoon garlic powder
2 cups sour cream
salt and pepper to taste
cooked fettuccini

Cook the cream cheese, cream and butter in a large saucepan over medium heat until the cream cheese and butter melt, stirring to mix well. Add the Parmesan cheese gradually, stirring after each addition until the cheese melts. Stir in the garlic powder, sour cream, salt and pepper. Add the fettuccini and toss to coat well.

For Shrimp Alfredo, sauté garlic to taste in ¾ cup butter in a skillet over medium heat. Add 1½ pounds shrimp and cook just until pink. Stir in the Alfredo sauce; toss with the fettuccini.

For Chicken Alfredo, sprinkle 3 chicken breasts on both sides with lemon pepper and grill until cooked through. Slice into thin strips. Add to the Alfredo sauce and simmer over low heat. Toss with the fettuccini.

Yields 6 servings

JOHN CREMEANS

Cremeans' Red Hot Pepper Chili

Coming from the far reaches of the north, New Richmond, Wisconsin (just outside of Minneapolis-St. Paul, Minnesota), you're always looking for ways to keep warm. In the Cremeans household, there's nothing better than sitting down to a nice hot bowl of chili and a cup of real cold buttermilk.

1½ pounds ground beef

1 envelope chili spice

2 (16-ounce) cans red
    kidney beans

2 (15-ounce) cans chili tomatoes

1 (16-ounce) can tomato sauce

1 medium onion, chopped

2 tablespoons red pepper flakes,
    or to taste

Brown the ground beef in a skillet, stirring until crumbly; drain well. Combine the ground beef, chili spice, beans, tomatoes, tomato sauce, onion and red pepper flakes in a large saucepan and mix well. Simmer for 3 hours.

Yields 6 servings

I love to cook! It's fun having friends and family over to the house and seeing them eat my creations.

John Cremeans

Cremeans' Classic
Hot and Spicy Bean Dip

I know that this appetizer recipe may seem way too easy, but you'll be amazed how many of your guests will love it. The thing with this recipe is that it gets hotter the more you eat, so make sure you have plenty of beverages around to quench the thirst of your guests. I've made this dip when having friends and family over for a night of grilled steak fajitas.

2 (16-ounce) cans refried
    beans with green chiles
    or jalapeños
1 cup chopped jalapeños

16 ounces shredded Cheddar
    cheese
12 ounces shredded 4-cheese
    Mexican blend

Beat the beans at high speed in a large microwave-safe mixer bowl until thin. Add the jalapeños. Microwave on High for 3 minutes; stir. Add the Cheddar cheese. Microwave for 4 minutes. Stir again and add the 4-cheese blend. Microwave for 3 minutes. Stir before serving. Serve with warm tortilla chips. The final microwaving step can be delayed until serving time.

    Yields 24 servings

When The Home Shopping Network went national in 1985, Dan Dennis was already one of its show hosts. Dan's drive for achievement goes back to his college days at Montclair State College in New Jersey, where he graduated with honors and a B.A. degree in Business and Marketing. At The Home Shopping Network, his expertise led to a stint in Scheduling; he has also served as an advisor on gemstones, collectibles, and other product lines.

Dan's Tropical Chicken

4 boneless skinless
    chicken breasts
¾ cup (about) orange juice
1 (8-ounce) can juice-pack
    pineapple chunks
¼ cup shredded coconut
chopped maraschino cherries
    to taste

1 to 2 tablespoons orange juice
1 tablespoon (about) honey
2 tablespoons (about) apricot
    or peach preserves
cooked rice
orange, lemon and lime slices
shredded coconut (optional)

Combine the chicken with ¾ cup orange juice or enough to cover in a shallow dish. Marinate chicken in the refrigerator for 1 to 2 hours. Drain. Discard the marinade.

Combine the undrained pineapple, ¼ cup coconut and cherries in a bowl. Stir in 1 to 2 tablespoons orange juice, honey and preserves, adjusting the amounts until the mixture is thick enough to coat the chicken.

Grill the chicken over medium coals until nearly cooked through. Cut evenly spaced slits into the chicken. Brush both sides of the chicken with the pineapple mixture. Grill until cooked through, turning and basting as needed.

Serve with rice and thin slices of orange, lemon and lime. Sprinkle with additional shredded coconut.

Yields 4 servings

DAN DENNIS

Dan's Carrot and Banana Supreme

1 tablespoon butter

¼ cup packed brown sugar

1 cup thinly sliced carrots

2 bananas, thickly sliced

½ teaspoon cinnamon

Heat the butter and brown sugar in a sauté pan until the butter is melted and the brown sugar is dissolved. Add the carrots. Sauté over low heat for 5 minutes or until the carrots are tender. Add the bananas. Sauté for 2 to 3 minutes or just until the bananas are heated through. Sprinkle with the cinnamon and serve immediately. May be served as a side dish or dessert.

Yields 4 servings

Dan's Homemade Slaw

8 ounces green cabbage

8 ounces red cabbage

2 carrots

1 onion

1 cup mayonnaise

4 teaspoons sugar

1 teaspoon garlic powder

salt and pepper to taste

1 cup drained fresh
    pineapple cubes

½ cup golden raisins

Cut the green cabbage, red cabbage, carrots and onion finely in a large bowl. Add the mayonnaise, sugar, garlic powder, salt and pepper and toss to mix. Add the pineapple and raisins and mix well. Anyone who has the "Smart Chopper" should use it for this recipe.

Yields 10 servings

Red Velvet Cake

This was one of my father's favorites. I found it again through Dottie, a Call Center representative.

2 eggs
1 cup vegetable oil
1½ cups sugar
1 teaspoon vinegar
1 teaspoon vanilla extract
2 small bottles of red
    food coloring
2½ cups flour

1 teaspoon baking cocoa
1 teaspoon baking soda
1 cup buttermilk
½ cup butter, softened
8 ounces cream cheese, softened
1 (16-ounce) package
    confectioners' sugar
1 cup chopped pecans

Beat the eggs, oil and sugar in a mixer bowl until frothy. Beat in the vinegar, vanilla and food coloring.

Mix the flour, baking cocoa and baking soda in a bowl. Add to the egg mixture alternately with the buttermilk, beating well after each addition.

Spoon into 2 greased and floured 9-inch cake pans. Bake at 350 degrees for 30 minutes. Cool in the pans for 10 minutes. Remove to a wire rack to cool completely.

Cream the butter and cream cheese in a mixer bowl. Add the confectioners' sugar gradually, beating until smooth. Spread the frosting between the layers and over the top and side of the cake. Press the pecans on the side of the cake.

Yields 16 servings

Tracey has been a show host at The Home Shopping Network since 1997. She earned a Bachelor's of Fine Arts in Theater from Northern Kentucky University. Her previous professional experience includes singing in a gospel group as a child, spending years acting in musical theater and commercials, and hosting on two other shopping channels. Tracey says, "The most important thing about being a host is that so many people are too busy to get out. I feel like I have thousands of shopping buddies."

TRACEY EDWARDS

Ruthie's Pineapple Upside-Down Cake

1 (20-ounce) can crushed
    pineapple
$\frac{1}{2}$ cup butter
$\frac{1}{2}$ cup packed brown sugar
$\frac{1}{3}$ cup sliced drained
    cherries

3 egg yolks
1$\frac{1}{4}$ cups sugar
1$\frac{1}{2}$ cups flour
1$\frac{1}{2}$ teaspoons baking powder
1 teaspoon vanilla extract
3 egg whites, stiffly beaten

Drain the pineapple, reserving $\frac{1}{2}$ cup of the juice. Heat the butter and brown sugar in an ovenproof skillet until the butter is melted and the brown sugar is dissolved. Stir in the cherries and pineapple.

    Combine the egg yolks, reserved pineapple juice, sugar, flour, baking powder and vanilla in a bowl and mix well. Fold in the egg whites. Spoon over the pineapple mixture.

    Bake at 325 degrees for 1 hour. Let cool in the skillet. Invert onto a serving plate.

    Yields 12 servings

My parents were the

county jailers in Burlington,

Kentucky. My father loved to

bake and was always in

direct competition with his

three sisters.

Aunt Margie's
Famous Yeast Rolls

2 envelopes dry yeast

1/2 cup warm water

1/4 cup butter-flavor shortening

1/2 cup sugar

2 teaspoons salt

1 1/2 cups 2% milk or whole
    milk, scalded

2 eggs, beaten

5 1/2 to 6 cups flour

1/4 cup melted butter

Dissolve the yeast in the warm water and set aside. Combine the shortening, sugar and salt in a large bowl. Pour the hot milk over the sugar mixture. Let stand until lukewarm. Add the eggs and yeast mixture and mix well. Mix in enough of the flour to make a soft dough. Place the dough in a greased bowl, turning to coat the surface. Let rise, covered, in a warm place until doubled in bulk. Roll on a floured surface. Cut with a round biscuit cutter or drinking glass. Place the rolls in a greased baking pan. Let rise, covered, until almost doubled in bulk. Bake at 375 degrees for 10 minutes or until golden brown. Brush the hot rolls with butter.

Yields 4 dozen

I remember coming home from school to freshly baked bread. We always had kitchen round table discussions over baked goods. This kept the family bickering to a minimum and made for very happy prisoners (at least in the sweet tooth department).

Su came to The Home Shopping Network in 1986. For her, the most important thing about being a show host is "being able to bring great value in to viewers' homes." Her previous selling experiences prepared her for selling the network's wide variety of products. Su says, "You name it; I've sold it." Today, Su says what she loves most about being a show host is "talking to the viewers, and I really enjoy the people here that I work with daily."

Mom Ferrera's Zucchini Bread

3 eggs

2 cups sugar

1 cup vegetable oil

1 tablespoon vanilla extract

2 cups all-purpose or whole
   wheat flour

¼ teaspoon baking powder

2 teaspoons baking soda

1 tablespoon cinnamon

2 teaspoons salt

2 cups loosely packed,
   coarsely grated zucchini

1 cup chopped walnuts

1 cup raisins

Beat the eggs in a mixer bowl until frothy. Add the sugar, oil and vanilla gradually, beating until thick and smooth. Add the flour, baking powder, baking soda, cinnamon and salt and mix well. Stir in the zucchini, walnuts and raisins.

Spoon into 2 greased and floured 4x8-inch loaf pans. Bake at 350 degrees for 1 hour. Remove to a wire rack to cool.

Yields 2 loaves

SU FERRERA

Potato Chip Cookies

3 cups flour, sifted

1$\frac{1}{2}$ cups crushed potato chips

2 cups butter, softened

1$\frac{1}{4}$ cups sugar

1 teaspoon vanilla extract

Mix the flour and potato chip crumbs in a medium bowl. Cream the butter, sugar and vanilla in a mixer bowl until smooth. Add the flour mixture and mix well. Drop by teaspoonfuls onto an ungreased cookie sheet. Bake at 350 degrees for 12 minutes. Cool on a wire rack.

Yields 7 dozen

I started out on The Home Shopping Network over 12 years ago. Not only has this become my career, it has also blessed me with some of the strongest friendships I've ever made in my life.

"...I've had the opportunity to work with some outstanding chefs..."

Su Ferrera

Easy Southern-Fried Catfish

2 eggs, or equivalent amount
    of egg substitute
2 tablespoons water
2 cups stone-ground white
    cornmeal

2 teaspoons salt
freshly ground pepper to taste
3 pounds catfish fillets
½ cup (about) shortening

Beat the eggs and water in a bowl. Combine the cornmeal, salt and pepper in a shallow dish and mix well. Dip the catfish into the egg mixture, then into the cornmeal mixture.

Heat the shortening in a heavy cast-iron skillet. Add the catfish. Fry until crusty and golden brown, turning once. Drain well before serving.

Yields 6 to 8 servings

I've had the opportunity to learn a lot of new skills, such as cooking. I've always enjoyed cooking in the past, but now doing many of our cooking shows, I've had the opportunity to work with some outstanding chefs and also with our very talented food stylists. I've certainly learned a lot from them!

Bill became a show host in 1997. Before that he was The Home Shopping Network's Director of Quality Assurance for Jewelry for three years. Bill previously held a number of managerial positions at a major jewelry corporation, where he worked for 16 years. What Bill likes most about being a show host, he says, is "meeting, entertaining, presenting products to people throughout the country and, of course, being on TV live!"

Grandma Rene's Homemade Baklava

My grandmother did not make this very often, but when she did, it was a very special treat. I used to watch in amazement as she prepared baklava. She had the ability to handle the phyllo dough which is very thin and often difficult to handle. She used to say it was worth every minute—of course, she never got an argument from anyone in the family. I promise you this, if you prepare this dessert, you will have experienced the highest level of indulgence!

8 ounces phyllo pastry sheets

8 ounces shelled pistachio
nuts, ground

3 tablespoons sugar

¾ teaspoon ground cinnamon

1½ tablespoons rose water

½ cup melted diet margarine

½ cup rose water syrup (found
in Mediterranean stores)

whole cloves (optional)

Cover the phyllo sheets with plastic wrap to prevent drying out. Combine the nuts, sugar, cinnamon and rose water in a small bowl and mix well. Place 3 phyllo sheets in a lightly greased 9x13-inch baking pan. Brush with melted margarine. Alternate layers of the nut mixture and 3 sheets of phyllo in the pan, brushing every third sheet of phyllo with butter and ending with phyllo. Cut the baklava diagonally at 1½-inch intervals to form 35 diamond shapes. Bake at 400 degrees for 15 minutes or until golden brown. Place on a wire rack to cool. Drizzle evenly with the rose water syrup. Let stand for several hours. Top each diamond shape with a whole clove.

Yields 35 pieces

BILL GREEN

I have always loved various

types of stir-fry dishes. One

day I was fooling around

in the kitchen, and I just

started to throw things into

a frying pan.

Chicken Vegetable Stir-Fry

This is now one of my own favorite stir-fry dishes. It is always dependable, satisfying, and fast to prepare—and everyone loves it. You can hit the grocery store and have this on the table in 45 minutes from start to finish. Ready, set, shop, and cook!

2 cups basmati rice
4 boneless skinless chicken
    breasts, cubed
3 tablespoons olive oil
2 tablespoons minced garlic
$\frac{1}{2}$ teaspoon pepper
1 yellow bell pepper,
    chopped
1 red bell pepper, chopped

8 ounces snap peas, stems
    removed
1 large sweet onion, chopped
8 ounces sliced mushrooms
1 or 2 carrots, shredded
4 ounces sliced water chestnuts
$\frac{3}{4}$ to 1 cup teriyaki marinade
2 cups chicken stock
2 tablespoons cornstarch
$\frac{1}{4}$ cup warm water

Prepare the rice using package directions. Stir-fry the chicken cubes in olive oil in a large skillet until golden brown and cooked through. Stir in the garlic and pepper. Add the yellow and red bell peppers, snap peas, onion, mushrooms, carrots and water chestnuts. Stir-fry for 4 to 5 minutes or until tender-crisp. Pour in the teriyaki marinade and chicken stock. Simmer, covered, for 10 minutes. Whisk the cornstarch and $\frac{1}{4}$ cup warm water in a small bowl. Stir into the chicken mixture. Simmer, covered, for 10 to 20 minutes. Serve over the rice.

Yields 6 to 8 servings

Momma Emily's Chicken Soup with Matzo Balls

This is a favorite traditional Jewish soup that has been served in most Jewish households throughout history during the Jewish holidays and for big family gatherings. But you certainly do not have to be Jewish to love this delicious and hearty soup.

4 eggs

2 egg whites

1 teaspoon salt

1½ cups matzo meal

3 tablespoons cold water

2 tablespoons vegetable oil

16 cups chicken broth

2 cups shredded or chopped
   cooked chicken

4 parsnips, peeled, chopped

6 carrots, peeled, chopped

2 large onions, chopped

2 cups broccoli florets

2 cups sliced mushrooms

¼ cup chopped fresh dillweed
   or parsley

I always teased my mom because she never made just enough for dinner. She always made enough to "feed an army." Years later I have lived to regret ever saying that—because soup freezes beautifully for months after Mom's visits.

Whisk the eggs, egg whites and salt in a bowl. Whisk in the matzo meal, cold water and oil until blended. Chill, covered, for 1 to 12 hours. (Double for additional matzo balls.)

Bring the broth to a boil in a stockpot. Add the chicken, parsnips, carrots and onions. Reduce the heat to medium-low. Cook for 3 minutes. Shape the chilled matzo dough by level teaspoonfuls into balls. Drop the balls immediately into the simmering broth. (The dough must be cold or the matzo balls will either fall apart or be rock-hard.) Cook, covered, for 15 minutes; do not peek. Add the broccoli and mushrooms. Simmer for 3 minutes or just until the broccoli is tender. Ladle into bowls. Sprinkle with the dillweed or parsley.

Yields 15 to 20 servings

June first worked for The Home Shopping Network in the summer of 1997, then came back to us in May of this year. June is a graduate of the University of Minnesota with a B.A. in Broadcast Journalism. She has a lot of experience in the television industry, having worked as a TV reporter, news anchor, producer, talk show host, and educational video producer/writer. When not hosting for The Home Shopping Network, June plans to write screenplays and a romance novel.

Chicken Paprikash Soup

Experiment with this recipe. Taste it as you go along, looking for a spicy full-bodied chicken flavor.

1 chicken, rinsed in cold
    water
1 large white onion, chopped
1½ teaspoons salt, or
    to taste
1½ teaspoons red pepper
    flakes
2 teaspoons paprika

1 or 2 chicken bouillon
    cubes, or 1 (10-ounce)
    can chicken broth
    (optional)
6 eggs, or equivalent egg
    substitute
1 teaspoon salt
2 cups (about) flour

Place the chicken and cold water to cover in a 6- to 8-quart Dutch oven. Add the next 4 ingredients. Bring to a boil. Simmer, covered, for at least 3 hours, making sure the chicken is cooked through. Shred or cut the chicken into bite-size pieces, discarding the skin and bones. Skim the broth. Add enough water to make 5 quarts of broth. Add the bouillon cubes. Add additional red pepper flakes and paprika sparingly to make broth spicy and red. Stir the chicken into the broth; bring to a boil. Beat the eggs and 1 teaspoon salt in a mixer bowl. Stir in the flour by tablespoonfuls until dough is stiff and sticky. Drop the dough by teaspoonfuls into the boiling broth. Cook for 2 minutes. Dumplings may sink first and then rise to the top when cooked.

Yields 8 servings

JUNE HAGMAN

DeHart's Midway-Style Barbecue Sauce

You can make a great North Carolina midway-style barbecue sandwich with this sauce. Just mix it with shredded barbecued or roasted pork or chicken. Add mayonnaise-based coleslaw to the sandwich to be really authentic.

1 (32-ounce) bottle catsup	2 tablespoons lemon juice
1¾ cups white vinegar	1 tablespoon salt
1¾ cups water	1½ teaspoons pepper
2 tablespoons sugar	1½ teaspoons red pepper flakes

Combine the catsup, vinegar, water, sugar, lemon juice, salt, pepper and red pepper flakes in a large saucepan and mix well. Bring almost to a rolling boil over medium to high heat, stirring frequently. Remove from heat. Let stand until cool.

Yields 2 quarts

I started cookbook and recipe collecting when I was a teenager and kept an elaborate file system that became way too cumbersome. Now, I just buy compilation cookbooks and an occasional women's club, church, or family cookbook.

June Hagman

Chinese Coleslaw

1 cup vegetable oil

3 tablespoons white
vinegar

3 tablespoons sugar

2 (3-ounce) packages
Oriental-flavored ramen
noodles, crumbled

1 (8-ounce) package
shredded cabbage with
carrots

1 small bunch green onions,
chopped

⅓ cup slivered almonds,
toasted

Whisk the oil, vinegar, sugar and ramen noodle seasonings in
a small bowl until mixed. Toss the cabbage, green onions and
almonds in a large bowl. Mix in the ramen noodles. Drizzle the
dressing over the salad and toss to mix well. Serve immediately.
For variety, use flavored vinegars in place of the white vinegar.

Serves 6

With two very active boys who love to snow ski and water ski and a husband who still plays rugby, we need nourishing meals that keep the energy level up! I try to make our family supper time special with place mats, the whole nine yards! It doesn't always happen, what with sports and work schedules, but this is our best time to catch up with each other about the day's activities.

Brian's professional experience makes him well qualified to assume the role of a show host specializing in fitness. Brian has a degree in exercise science and is a member of the American College of Sports Medicine. He is a Certified Fitness Trainer with the International Sportscience Association and appeared on America's Health Network for two years. He joined The Home Shopping Network in 1997. Brian says what he likes most about his new job are "helping people and the rush of energy I get before every show."

Greek Macaroni Salad

¼ cup olive oil

2 tablespoons lemon juice

2 tablespoons vinegar

1 teaspoon oregano

½ teaspoon salt

⅛ teaspoon pepper

1 clove of garlic, crushed

1 teaspoon dillweed

1 large tomato, finely chopped

1 cup finely chopped
 green bell pepper

½ onion, finely chopped

½ cup shredded Cheddar cheese

½ cup pitted whole black olives

1 (12-ounce) package macaroni,
 cooked and cooled

Combine the olive oil, lemon juice, vinegar, oregano, salt, pepper, garlic and dillweed in a small bowl and mix well.

Combine the tomato, green pepper, onion, cheese, black olives and cooked macaroni in a large bowl and mix well. Add the olive oil mixture. Toss to coat. Refrigerate, covered, until ready to serve.

Yields 2 quarts

BRIAN HYDER

Easy Layered Spaghetti

12 ounces spaghetti

1 pound ground beef

1 (48-ounce) jar spaghetti
 sauce

1 (14-ounce) jar spaghetti
 sauce

1 teaspoon salt

1 teaspoon sugar

3 cups shredded
 mozzarella cheese

8 ounces cream cheese, softened

1 cup sour cream

¾ cup shredded
 Cheddar cheese

¾ cup shredded Monterey
 Jack cheese

Cook the spaghetti in boiling water in a saucepan for 10 minutes; drain. Brown the ground beef in a skillet, stirring until crumbly; drain. Stir in all the spaghetti sauce, salt and sugar. Simmer until heated through, stirring frequently.

Combine the mozzarella cheese, cream cheese and sour cream in a bowl and mix well. Layer the ground beef mixture, spaghetti and sour cream mixture one-half at a time in a baking dish. Sprinkle with the Cheddar cheese and Monterey Jack cheese.

Bake at 350 degrees for 45 minutes or until brown and bubbly. Add sliced mushrooms if desired.

Yields 8 servings

When I was a child and

curious about the wonders

of the kitchen, I got up

early one morning and

decided to cook breakfast for

my parents. I thought, how

hard can it be?

Brian Hyder

My first experience in The Home Shopping Network kitchen was early one morning when we sold out of the jewelry scheduled for the show. We were moved to the kitchen set to present Farberware: a toaster, a can opener, and a mixer with a bowl—nice products that my producer assured me would sell themselves. All I had to do was introduce the products. I put a bagel in the toaster and pushed the knob down. Nothing happened! I saw that the elements were not heating, so I reset it on dark and moved to the can opener to give the toaster time to heat up. I put a can of soup in the opener and pushed the handle down. Nothing happened! I repositioned the can and tried once more. Nothing happened! Now my producer is laughing, "Brian, don't you know how to open a can of soup?" In a panic, it suddenly dawned on me that we had no power. I signaled to my floor man John that the extension cord was not plugged in, and I moved to the mixer to buy time. The viewers got a detailed description of the icing ingredients in the mixer bowl. Then John gave me the "thumbs up." I turned the mixer on low. Nothing happened! On high. Nothing happened! John ran in and wiggled the mixer's plug. Something happened! The mixer blades were upright and full of raw eggs and flour—food was slung all over the set. As I scrambled to shut off the mixer, the can opener was opening the can. As I ran to the opener, the can dropped down on the counter. Then I realized the bagel in the toaster was on fire. As I ran to it, the bagel ejected from the toaster into the camera lens. Everyone was laughing hard at my antics. My producer was right: Farberware really does sell itself. We sold a record number that morning.

I have seen my mom cook our breakfast. She just cracks a few eggs, pops a couple of tarts in the toaster, chops some potatoes, puts them in the pan with eggs, and "voila!"—breakfast.

Two hours, 12 eggs, several potatoes, and one box of tarts later, I proudly served my parents a fine breakfast of peanut butter and jelly on burnt toast. I did get the o.j. right. Fortunately, I went from my mother's kitchen to my wife's without having to learn any more than the original recipe I perfected that early morning.

Fruit Pizza

½ cup confectioners' sugar
¾ cup margarine, softened
1½ cups flour
8 ounces reduced-fat cream
    cheese, softened
1¼ cups sugar
1 teaspoon vanilla extract

fruit (blueberries, bananas,
    kiwifruit, orange slices,
    pineapple, strawberries)
2½ tablespoons cornstarch
1 cup fruit juice
1 teaspoon lemon juice

Combine the confectioners' sugar, margarine and flour in a bowl and mix well. Pat into a pizza pan. Bake at 300 degrees for 10 to 15 minutes or until golden brown; do not overbake. Beat the cream cheese, ½ cup of the sugar and the vanilla in a bowl until smooth. Spread the cream cheese mixture over the crust. Arrange fruit over the cream cheese mixture. Combine the cornstarch, fruit juice, remaining ¾ cup sugar and lemon juice in a saucepan and mix well. Bring to a boil. Boil until slightly thick. Let stand until cool. Pour evenly over pizza.

Yields 8 to 10 servings

MICHELE LAU

Turkey Salad

This salad is great for summertime picnics, class reunions, and the like. It is also a good way to use leftovers.

2 quarts chopped cooked turkey	3 to 4 cups mayonnaise
1 quart chopped celery	3 cups seedless green grapes
1 (12-ounce) bottle Italian salad dressing	salt and pepper to taste
Garlic powder to taste	1 cup slivered almonds, toasted

Combine the turkey and celery in a large bowl and mix well. Add the salad dressing, tossing to coat. Season with garlic powder. Marinate, covered, in the refrigerator for 8 to 10 hours; drain. Add the mayonnaise, grapes, salt and pepper to the turkey mixture and mix well. Store, covered, in the refrigerator. Mix in the almonds just before serving.

Yields 20 servings

My recipe book is like a patchwork quilt—my mind wanders to the backyard barbecues, roommates, and dinner parties of the past. In creating these recipes, I can literally taste the times of my life once more.

Michele Lau

Minnesota Wild Rice Soup

1 cup Minnesota wild rice

1½ ribs celery, chopped

1 large onion, chopped

½ green bell pepper, chopped

8 ounces fresh mushrooms, sliced

½ cup butter

½ cup flour

8 cups chicken broth

salt and pepper to taste

1 cup half-and-half

3 tablespoons dry white wine

I hope that these recipes bring you and yours as much joy as they have mine. A recipe is much like a good meal: It is so much better when it is shared.

Rinse the rice and cook using the package directions. Sauté the celery, onion, green bell pepper and mushrooms in the butter in a large saucepan until tender. Add the flour gradually, stirring constantly until mixed; do not brown. Stir in the broth. Add the rice, salt and pepper and mix well. Cook just until heated through, stirring frequently. Stir in the half-and-half. Cook just until heated through. Mix in the white wine just before serving.

Yields 6 servings

Colleen came to The Home Shopping Network in 1993. She has worked in television for 12 years, previously hosting two talk shows in Minneapolis and working as a consumer reporter for four years. She also spent three years at the CVN shopping network in Minneapolis. About working at The Home Shopping Network, Colleen says, "I love the excitement of live TV. I love the challenge of selling great products. I love the people I get to meet on the air everyday!"

Christmas Crazy Crunch

2 quarts lightly salted
    popped corn
1⅓ cups pecans
⅔ cup almonds

1½ cups sugar
1 cup butter or margarine
½ cup light corn syrup
1 teaspoon vanilla extract

Combine the popped corn, pecans and almonds on a baking sheet and mix well. Combine the sugar, butter and corn syrup in a saucepan. Cook over medium heat until boiling, stirring constantly. Boil for 10 to 25 minutes or until the mixture turns a light caramel color, stirring occasionally. Remove from heat. Stir in the vanilla. Pour over the popped corn mixture. Mix to coat well. Spread out to dry. Break apart. Store in a tightly covered container.

Yields 2½ quarts

COLLEEN LOPEZ

White Chili

8 boneless skinless chicken breast halves

4 cups chicken stock

1 (4-ounce) can chopped green chiles, or to taste

1 small onion, chopped

1 large clove of garlic, minced

2 (16-ounce) cans Great Northern beans

tortilla chips

Grill the chicken over hot coals until cooked through. Slice into thin strips. Combine the chicken, stock, chiles, onion and garlic in a stockpot. Bring to a boil; reduce heat. Simmer over medium heat for 15 minutes, stirring occasionally. Stir in the beans. Simmer for 10 minutes longer or until heated through, stirring occasionally. Ladle into chili bowls. Serve with tortilla chips.

Yields 6 to 8 servings

We love experimenting with new chili recipes at our house. One of my family's favorites is this white chili recipe I learned from a good friend from Minnesota—it's super easy and, oh, so good!

Colleen Lopez

Colleen's Mexican Lasagna

1 pound lean ground beef

1 (16-ounce) can refried
    beans

1 small onion, finely chopped

1 clove of garlic, minced

½ teaspoon chili powder

12 corn tortillas, cut into
    strips

¼ cup vegetable oil

1 cup shredded Colby cheese

1 cup shredded Monterey Jack
    cheese

1 cup shredded Cheddar cheese

2 (10-ounce) cans enchilada
    sauce

My husband's family cooks a lot of authentic Mexican dishes. Here is a recipe I learned from my sister-in-law that is easy and delicious! (P.S.—You can use your own homemade enchilada sauce, but for a shortcut, I use premade sauce from the grocery store!)

Brown the ground beef in a skillet, stirring until crumbly; drain. Stir in the beans, onion, garlic and chili powder. Cook just until heated through, stirring frequently.

Fry the tortilla strips in the oil in a skillet until brown on both sides; drain. Combine the Colby cheese, Monterey Jack cheese and Cheddar cheese in a bowl and mix well.

Spread 2 tablespoons of the enchilada sauce over the bottom of a greased lasagna pan. Layer the tortilla strips, ground beef mixture, remaining enchilada sauce and cheese mixture ⅓ at a time in the prepared pan. Bake at 350 degrees for 35 minutes. Let stand for 15 minutes before serving.

Yields 4 to 6 servings

Heidi Lyon has been around...around the Caribbean, that is, working as a port lecturer on cruise ships. She managed to continue exercising her spirit of adventure by becoming a show host for The Home Shopping Network in 1997. Most important to Heidi is the chance she has "to talk to and meet people across the country." She says one of her favorite aspects of show hosting is "the opportunity to talk ALL the time."

Trifle

1 (12-count) package sponge
cake jelly rolls
sherry (optional)
1 (15-ounce) can fruit
cocktail, drained
1 (3-ounce) package red
gelatin

1 (4-ounce) package low-fat
instant vanilla pudding or
custard mix
1 envelope light whipped
topping mix

Cut the jelly rolls into ½-inch slices. Arrange the slices cut side out along the bottom and side of a trifle bowl. Drizzle sherry over the slices. Arrange the fruit cocktail evenly over the slices.

Prepare the gelatin using package directions. Pour over the fruit cocktail. Chill in the refrigerator until the gelatin is set. Prepare the pudding mix using package directions. Pour over the gelatin. Chill until set. Prepare the whipped topping using package directions. Spread over the pudding. Garnish with mandarin orange segments and raspberries.

Yields 8 to 10 servings

HEIDI LYON

Now, I am the first one to

admit that I made mistakes.

I confused baking powder

and baking soda and made

the most revolting muffins

you have ever tasted!

Chicken Divan

2 stalks fresh broccoli

6 boneless skinless chicken
    breasts, poached,
    chopped

2 (10-ounce) cans cream of
    chicken soup

1 cup mayonnaise

1 teaspoon lemon juice

$\frac{1}{4}$ teaspoon curry powder

$\frac{1}{2}$ cup shredded cheese

$\frac{1}{2}$ cup bread crumbs

1 tablespoon melted butter

Steam the broccoli in a steamer for 10 minutes. Drain and coarsely chop. Arrange the broccoli in a large baking dish. Top with the chicken. Combine the soup, mayonnaise, lemon juice and curry powder in a bowl and mix well. Spoon over the chicken. Sprinkle with the cheese. Combine the bread crumbs and butter in a small bowl. Sprinkle over the top. Bake at 350 degrees for 20 to 25 minutes or until brown and bubbly.

Yields 4 to 6 servings

I was never a big cook until I moved to Florida and joined The Home Shopping Network. I grew up in southern Ontario, and my mom is an excellent cook. My friends always wanted to come to my house for Sunday dinner, because amazing roast beef and Yorkshire pudding was always accompanied by three kinds of potatoes, five kinds of vegetables, and a killer salad. My mom always thought she was cooking for 12, instead of the four or five of us who were home for dinner. By the time I was in university, I was working at one restaurant or another, and I constantly ate at work rather than cooking for myself. And, then, three years on cruise ships had me eating in the Officer's Mess off a menu...with waiters and busboys!

It wasn't until I moved to Florida that I realized, not only did I not know how to cook, but I had nothing to cook with. In all honesty, I talked myself into a lot of our "easy, goof-proof" items from The Home Shopping Network and now own a bread maker (yes, I make my own pizza now) and the George Foreman Grill. I also have the Smart Chopper (and I make my own salsa and tuna salad), the Spanek Chicken Roaster (it's so-o-o easy), and the Ultrex (long live the Ultrex). Thanks to the very patient tutelage of fellow host Su Ferrera and our food stylist Debbie, I am not only daring with my cooking... I am really enjoying it!

Then I forgot to plug in my Crock-Pot and almost served raw meatballs. And, being Canadian, I mixed up the entire Celsius vs. Fahrenheit concept and completely charbroiled my first chicken—it looked like charcoal.

Barbara's varied professional experiences gave her the flexibility needed to become a show host on The Home Shopping Network in 1992. Before that, Barbara worked in banking, insurance, apartment management, interior design, international marketing, and sales. Show host Alice Cleveland convinced Barbara to take a screen test. Barbara says what is most important to her about show hosting is "connecting with the viewer—relating to what we have in common."

Rush Hour Chicken

½ cup flour
1 teaspoon lemon pepper
1 teaspoon garlic powder
4 to 6 chicken breasts
¼ cup butter

1 (15-ounce) can crushed
   tomatoes
1 green bell pepper, sliced
1 onion, sliced
½ cup sliced mushrooms

Combine the flour, lemon pepper and garlic powder in a shallow dish. Dredge the chicken breasts in the flour mixture, coating both sides. Melt the butter in a large skillet. Add the chicken. Brown the chicken on both sides. Add the tomatoes, green bell pepper, onion and mushrooms. Simmer for 30 to 45 minutes or until the chicken is cooked through.

Yields 4 to 6 servings

BARBARA MARVILLE

Easy Lemon-Garlic Grouper

½ cup (about) melted butter ¼ cup fresh lemon juice

4 teaspoons minced garlic 4 teaspoons paprika

4 grouper fillets

Pour the butter into a baking dish, tilting the dish to coat evenly. Spread 1 teaspoon garlic over the top and bottom of each fillet. Arrange the fillets in the prepared baking dish. Drizzle with the lemon juice and sprinkle with the paprika. Broil for 5 minutes; turn. Broil for 5 minutes longer or until the fish flakes easily. May substitute your favorite fish for the grouper.

Yields 4 servings

Going back a few years, I joined a health club and attended one of my first Tai Chi classes. The instructor, who also was the director of the club, was very charming.

Barbara Marville

Kelly's Carrot Cake

2 cups flour
2 cups sugar
1 teaspoon baking powder
1 teaspoon baking soda
1 teaspoon cinnamon
3 cups finely shredded carrots
1 cup vegetable oil

4 eggs
½ cup drained crushed
    pineapple
½ cup shredded coconut
¼ to ½ cup raisins
¼ to ½ cup chopped walnuts
Cream Cheese Frosting

Mix the flour, sugar, baking powder, baking soda and cinnamon in a mixer bowl. Add the carrots, oil, eggs, pineapple, coconut, raisins and walnuts. Beat until mixed, scraping the bowl occasionally. Spoon into 2 greased and floured 9-inch round cake pans. Bake at 350 degrees for 30 minutes or until the layers test done. Cool in pans for 10 minutes. Invert onto a wire rack to cool completely. Spread the Cream Cheese Frosting between the layers and over the top and side of the cake.

Yields 12 servings

Cream Cheese Frosting

16 ounces cream cheese,
    softened
1 cup butter, softened

4 teaspoons vanilla extract
8 to 9 cups sifted
    confectioners' sugar

Combine the cream cheese, butter and vanilla in a mixer bowl. Beat at high speed until creamy. Add the confectioners' sugar gradually, beating constantly until of a spreading consistency.

At my first class, I met a very special lady, Bea, a viewer of The Home Shopping Network. We hit it off great! I didn't know that she was the mother of the cute instructor of our class.

Well, lo and behold, over several months she encouraged her son to call me. She was doing her very best at playing "Cupid," and of course, it worked. Kelly and I are an item, best of friends, and we'll be setting a wedding date, hopefully in the near future.

81

Terry has been a show host for The Home Shopping Network since 1988. She earned a Bachelor of Arts in Journalism from the University of South Carolina, and her academic and leadership achievements placed her in Who's Who among Students in American Colleges and Universities. Terry has built her career in television, working as a news anchor, news reporter, and an editorial assistant in various markets. For Terry, what makes show hosting exciting is "direct daily contact with the customer."

Herb-Roasted Vegetables

3 sweet potatoes
1 red bell pepper
1 yellow bell pepper
1 red onion
8 ounces asparagus
8 cloves of garlic,
    coarsely chopped

1 1/2 teaspoons chopped
    fresh rosemary
1 teaspoon fresh thyme
2 tablespoons olive oil
1/2 teaspoon salt

Cut the sweet potatoes into halves lengthwise and then into 1/2-inch slices. Cut the red and yellow bell peppers and onion into 1x2-inch wedges. Cut the asparagus into 1-inch lengths. Place the vegetables in a large bowl. Add the garlic, rosemary, thyme and olive oil. Stir to coat the vegetables evenly. Arrange the vegetables on a baking sheet. Sprinkle with salt. Bake at 500 degrees for 18 to 20 minutes or until the vegetables are tender.

Yields 8 servings

TERRY LEWIS MASON

Grilled Salmon on a Bed of Spinach

10 ounces trimmed fresh
    spinach or 16 ounces
    loose fresh spinach
1 small clove of garlic,
    minced

2 teaspoons chopped fresh
    tarragon
1 (18-ounce) skinless
    salmon fillet

Rinse the spinach; do not drain. Combine the spinach, garlic and tarragon in a saucepan. Cook, covered, over medium heat for several minutes or just until the spinach wilts; drain. Cover and keep warm. Grill the salmon over hot coals or broil for 8 to 10 minutes per inch or until the salmon flakes easily. Arrange the spinach on a serving platter. Top with the salmon.

Yields 3 servings

Terry Lewis Mason

Black Bean, Corn and Tomato Salad

4 cups fresh or thawed
   frozen corn kernels
4 cups canned black beans,
   rinsed, drained
4 cups coarsely chopped
   tomatoes

4 scallions, thinly sliced
4 teaspoons minced fresh
   jalapeños, or to taste
Lime and Cilantro Dressing

Combine the corn, black beans, tomatoes, scallions and jalapeños in a bowl and mix well. Add the Lime and Cilantro Dressing, tossing gently to coat. Store, covered, in the refrigerator until serving time.

Yields 8 servings

Lime and Cilantro Dressing

2 teaspoons ground cumin
$\frac{1}{2}$ cup fresh lime juice
$\frac{1}{4}$ cup vegetable oil

$\frac{1}{2}$ cup chopped fresh cilantro
1 teaspoon salt

Place the cumin in a small skillet. Cook over low heat for 1 minute or just until the skillet is warm and the cumin is heated through. Remove from heat. Stir in the lime juice, oil, cilantro and salt and mix well.

Mindy holds a degree in Radio and Television. She worked in radio and television news prior to coming to The Home Shopping Network. She began her career at The Home Shopping Network in 1987, left in 1994, and returned in 1998. Mindy has two sons, Dylan, age 7½, and Connor, age 6. Mindy's hobbies include eating, reading, playing piano, traveling, and working out. She loves food made with fresh ingredients.

Grandma Aggie's Cannoli Cake

1 (2-layer) package yellow cake mix

1 pound ricotta cheese

1 tablespoon orange juice

1 teaspoon vanilla extract

3 ounces chocolate shavings

1 cup chopped walnuts

3 ounces rum (optional)

¼ cup confectioners' sugar

Prepare and bake the cake mix using package directions. Cut each layer into halves horizontally to make 4 layers. Combine the ricotta cheese, orange juice, vanilla, 2 ounces of the chocolate shavings, walnuts, rum and confectioners' sugar in a bowl and mix well. Spread equal portions of the filling between the cake layers. Top the cake with additional confectioners' sugar and the remaining chocolate shavings.

Yields 12 to 16 servings

MINDY McCORTNEY

Mindy's Chicken Raspberry Salad

4 boneless skinless chicken breasts, grilled, cut into strips

1 head lettuce, torn into bite-size pieces

³/₄ cup chopped walnuts

3 or 4 ribs celery, chopped

¹/₂ cup chopped red onion

6 ounces fresh raspberries

3 to 5 ounces goat cheese, crumbled

¹/₂ cup olive oil

¹/₄ cup red wine vinegar

Combine the chicken, lettuce, walnuts, celery and onion in a large salad bowl and mix well. Add the raspberries and goat cheese and toss gently. Drizzle with a mixture of the olive oil and vinegar. Serve chilled.

Yields 6 servings

In my family, we try to get together for family time, and it often centers around food, because we all love to eat! At my house, we often hang out around the kitchen. I am known for my salads—nothing difficult, but tasty!

Mindy McCartney

Grandma Marge's Chocolate Cake

2¾ cups flour

½ cup baking cocoa

2 teaspoons baking soda

½ teaspoon salt

2 cups sugar

¾ cup shortening

1 cup buttermilk

2 eggs

1 cup boiling water

German Chocolate Frosting

Combine the flour, baking cocoa, baking soda and salt in a bowl and mix well. Combine the sugar and shortening in a mixer bowl. Beat until creamy, scraping the bowl occasionally. Add the buttermilk and eggs, beating well. Add the flour mixture one-half at a time and mix well. Stir in the boiling water. Spoon the batter into 2 greased 8- or 9-inch round cake pans. Bake at 350 degrees for 40 to 45 minutes or until the layers test done. Cool in pans for 10 minutes. Invert onto a wire rack to cool completely. Spread the chilled German Chocolate Frosting between the layers and over the top and side of the cake.

Yields 12 servings

German Chocolate Frosting

1 cup sugar

½ cup evaporated milk

½ cup margarine

3 egg yolks, lightly beaten

1 teaspoon vanilla extract

1 cup shredded coconut

1 cup chopped walnuts

Combine the sugar, evaporated milk, margarine, egg yolks and vanilla in a saucepan. Cook over medium heat for 12 minutes, stirring constantly. Remove from heat. Stir in the coconut and walnuts. Chill, covered, in the refrigerator.

89

The job of show host seems tailor-made for Lynn Murphy, who came to The Home Shopping Network in 1992. She holds a degree in Radio and Television and has wanted to be in entertainment as long as she can remember. Before coming to The Home Shopping Network, Lynn taught gymnastics for five years and was an office manager in construction sales for three years. With her show host job, Lynn says, "Everything fell into place." She adds, "I love making people happy! I love presenting a great value."

String Pie

1 pound ground beef
1/2 cup chopped onion
1/4 cup chopped green bell
   pepper (optional)
1 (15 1/2-ounce) jar spaghetti
   sauce
8 ounces hot cooked
   spaghetti

1/3 cup grated Parmesan
   cheese
2 eggs, beaten
2 teaspoons butter
1 cup cottage cheese
1/2 cup shredded mozzarella
   cheese

Brown the ground beef with the onion and green bell pepper in a large skillet, stirring until the ground beef is crumbly; drain. Stir in the spaghetti sauce. Combine the spaghetti, Parmesan cheese, eggs and butter in a large bowl and mix well. Arrange in a 9x13-inch baking pan. Spread the cottage cheese over the spaghetti layer. Spoon the ground beef mixture over the cottage cheese. Sprinkle the mozzarella cheese over the top. Bake at 350 degrees for 20 minutes or until the cheese melts.

Yields 6 to 8 servings

LYNN MURPHY

Murphy's Artichoke Dip

1 (8-ounce) can chopped
   artichokes in water,
   drained
$\frac{2}{3}$ cup mayonnaise

1 or 2 cloves of garlic,
   chopped
1 cup grated Parmesan
   cheese

Combine the artichokes, mayonnaise, garlic and half the cheese in a bowl and mix well. Spoon into a baking dish. Sprinkle with the remaining cheese. Bake at 350 degrees for 15 minutes or until bubbly.

Yields 8 servings

When it comes to cooking,

I am not the most creative

chef in the world. However,

I love recipes, especially my

mom's and my friends'; I

chose some of my favorites

to share with you. You'll

find these easy and delicious.

"...think of me when cooking
up something special for...
those you love."

Lynn Murphy

Uncle Moe's South Philly Meatballs

Great for parties and great to freeze for future use.

1 loaf Italian bread, torn into
    bite-size pieces
5 to 6 pounds ground beef
1 pound ground pork
6 eggs, lightly beaten
    (1 egg to every
    1 pound meat)
2 medium onions, minced

3 to 5 cloves of garlic,
    chopped
6 tablespoons grated
    Parmesan cheese
5 teaspoons salt
4 teaspoons pepper
1 tablespoon oregano
1 tablespoon basil

With crazy schedules, it's difficult to find time to cook; however, there is nothing quite like homemade yummy favorites that the whole family can enjoy. Have fun and think of me when cooking up something special for yourself and those you love!

Soak the bread in water to cover in a bowl. Squeeze the moisture from the bread. Combine the bread, ground beef, ground pork, eggs, onions, garlic, cheese, salt, pepper, oregano and basil in a bowl and mix well. Shape the mixture into meatballs using a small to medium scoop. Arrange the meatballs on greased baking sheets. Bake at 350 degrees for 30 to 35 minutes or until the ground beef and ground pork are cooked through, turning once or twice; drain.

Yields 7 to 7½ dozen meatballs

Atonia became a show host at The Home Shopping Network in 1997. She attended the Fashion Institute of Technology in New York. Her career began in fashion, then moved to modeling in print, acting in commercials, and doing voice-overs. Atonia loves practically everything about being a show host; she says she likes "preparing for the show, learning the product, giving the presentation, and receiving a phone call, which means somebody's watching!"

Mrs. Toombs' Peach Cobbler

6 to 8 peaches	1 egg, beaten
1½ cups packed brown sugar	2 teaspoons baking powder
1 cup water	1 cup flour
3 tablespoons butter, softened	¼ teaspoon salt
	½ cup milk

Peel the peaches and remove the pits. Cut the peaches into small pieces. Combine the peaches, 1¼ cups of the brown sugar and water in a baking pan. Bake, tightly covered, for 20 to 25 minutes or until tender. Cream the butter and remaining ¼ cup brown sugar in a bowl until smooth. Add the egg; mix well. Sift the baking powder, flour and salt together. Add the flour mixture and milk alternately to the creamed mixture, mixing well after each addition. Spoon the batter over the hot peaches. Bake at 375 degrees for 30 to 35 minutes or until golden brown.

Yields 6 to 8 servings

ATONIA PETTIFORD

Blanche Pettiford's Shrimp Orange Salad

1 pound shrimp, steamed, peeled, chilled
1 cup chopped celery
sections of 3 oranges

2 teaspoons chopped onion
$\frac{1}{2}$ cup low-fat mayonnaise
lettuce leaves

Combine the shrimp, celery, orange sections and onion in a bowl and mix gently. Stir in the mayonnaise and mix well. Spoon onto a lettuce-lined serving platter. May substitute thawed frozen cooked shrimp for the fresh shrimp.

Yields 6 servings

Blanche Pettiford's Peach Dessert

1 (15-ounce) can peach
    halves, drained
1 cup vanilla wafer crumbs

whipped cream
walnut halves

Roll the peach halves in the vanilla wafer crumbs in a shallow dish. Arrange the peach halves cut side down in dessert goblets. Top with whipped cream and walnut halves.

    Yields 5 to 6 servings

    Low-Fat Substitutions: Lighten the calories by using low-fat or fat-free vanilla wafer crumbs and low-fat whipped topping.

Chris became a show host in 1990. For Chris, the most important thing about being a host is "performing a service to our customers who can't get out or are too busy to shop." She became a show host because "I love people, being in the TV industry, and shopping!" Her professional experience includes nine years in the home shopping industry and five years at a local TV station in Oklahoma City. What does she like most about the job? "Our viewers!"

Blueberry Buckle Dessert

One of our favorite treats at Thanksgiving and Christmas was my mother's Blueberry Buckle Dessert. Mom got this recipe from her grandmother, my great-grandmother Marietta.

1 (15-ounce) can blueberries	½ cup chopped pecans
1 (20-ounce) can crushed pineapple	1 (6-ounce) package cherry gelatin
1 (6-ounce) package blueberry gelatin	4 ounces whipped topping chopped pecans
2 bananas, sliced	

Drain the blueberries and pineapple, reserving the juices. Prepare the blueberry gelatin using package directions, substituting the reserved blueberry juice and water for the water quantity. Pour the gelatin into a trifle bowl. Chill until set. Layer the blueberries, pineapple, bananas and ½ cup pecans over the gelatin. Prepare the cherry gelatin using package directions, substituting the reserved pineapple juice and water for the water quantity. Pour over the fruit. Chill until set. Spread the whipped topping over the top. Top with pecans.

Yields 10 servings

Variation: Set aside ¼ cup of the reserved blueberry juice. Prepare the gelatins as given above and pour into a 9x13-inch dish. Chill until the gelatin mounds. Stir in the fruits and pecans. Chill until set. Mix the whipped topping and the ¼ cup blueberry juice in a bowl. Spread over the top.

CHRIS SCANLON

Pretzel Salad

2 cups coarsely chopped
  pretzels
¾ cup melted butter
3 tablespoons sugar
8 ounces cream cheese,
  softened
1 cup sugar

4 ounces whipped topping
2 (3-ounce) packages
  strawberry gelatin
2 cups boiling water
2 (10-ounce) packages
  frozen strawberries,
  sweetened

Combine the pretzels, butter and 3 tablespoons sugar in a bowl and mix well. Pat over the bottom of a 9x13-inch baking pan. Bake at 400 degrees for 8 minutes. Let stand until cool. Beat the cream cheese and 1 cup sugar in a mixer bowl until creamy, scraping the bowl occasionally. Fold in the whipped topping. Spread over the baked layer. Dissolve the gelatin in the boiling water in a bowl and mix well. Stir in the strawberries. Chill until partially set. Spread over the cream cheese mixture. Chill until set.

Yields 8 to 10 servings

This salad is a favorite of my Oklahoma City Epic Lunch Bunch, a group of actresses that have been my friends since I was 16 years old. There are about 25 of us that try to get together at least twice a year for special occasions.

Chris Scanton

Buttermilk Fudge

This is just my favorite fudge recipe.

¼ cup butter

2 cups sugar

2 tablespoons light corn syrup

1 cup buttermilk

1 teaspoon baking soda

1 cup chopped pecans

Heat the butter in a saucepan until melted. Stir in the sugar and corn syrup. Add a mixture of the buttermilk and baking soda and mix well. Bring to a boil. Cook to 234 to 240 degrees on a candy thermometer, soft-ball stage, stirring constantly. Remove from heat. Let stand for 5 minutes. Beat until the mixture thickens and loses its luster. Stir in the pecans. Drop by spoonfuls onto waxed paper or pour into a buttered dish.

Yields 1½ pounds

My husband and I married just 27 days after meeting each other. He swept me off my feet. On our first date, we said we wanted to travel for the first 1½ years then have our first child, then get a house, and finally have our second child and live happily ever after. So far, we're right on schedule. I'm glad I'm able to share our recipes, my family, and stories with you, because all of our viewers are like family to me.

101

Joe became a show host in October of 1997. Joe enjoys being a show host, especially "The pure fun of it!" If you wonder how Joe knows so much about so many different things, consider that his past career has included stints as "weatherman, newsman, disc jockey, electronic salesman, TV producer and writer."

Baby Vegetables with Pasta

2 cloves of garlic, minced
2 tablespoons olive oil
2 pounds assorted baby
   vegetables

1 pound ziti, cooked
Fresh Herb Sauce
3 tablespoons grated Parmesan
   cheese

Cook the garlic in the olive oil in a saucepan over low heat for 10 minutes. Skewer the vegetables and brush with the garlic mixture. Grill over hot coals for 15 minutes or until the vegetables begin to brown, turning occasionally. Combine the ziti and Fresh Herb Sauce in a bowl and toss to coat. Place the pasta on plates and arrange the grilled vegetables over the pasta. Top with the cheese.

Yields 8 servings

Fresh Herb Sauce

1 teaspoon olive oil
1 tablespoon lemon juice
1 teaspoon grated lemon
   rind
1 tablespoon (heaping)
   chopped fresh chives

2 tablespoons (heaping) each
   chopped fresh Italian parsley
   and basil
1 tablespoon fresh thyme leaves
salt and freshly ground pepper
   to taste

Heat the olive oil in a saucepan; do not let it smoke. Remove from heat. Add the remaining ingredients and mix well.

JOE SHEEHAN

Roasted Acorn Squash with Wild Rice Salad

3 medium acorn squash, cut lengthwise into halves
6 tablespoons maple syrup
1½ cups wild rice
4½ cups vegetable broth or water
½ teaspoon salt
½ cup hazelnuts

2 tablespoons currants
¼ cup (heaping) minced fresh chives
juice of ½ orange
⅛ teaspoon white wine vinegar or Champagne vinegar
¼ teaspoon ginger

Arrange the squash halves cut side up on a baking sheet. Spray with nonstick olive oil spray. Bake at 350 degrees for 1 hour or until tender. Drizzle 1 tablespoon of the maple syrup over each squash half.

For the wild rice, rinse the rice in a colander and drain. Bring the broth and salt to a boil in a saucepan. Add the rice; reduce the heat. Simmer, covered, for 35 to 40 minutes or until the rice is tender; drain. Let stand until cool.

Spread the hazelnuts on a baking sheet. Toast at 350 degrees for 7 minutes. Rub off the skins and chop coarsely.

Toss the rice, hazelnuts, currants and chives in a large bowl. Whisk the orange juice, vinegar and ginger in a small bowl. Drizzle over the rice mixture and mix well. Serve with the squash.

Yields 6 servings

Joe Sheehan

Apricot, Mango and Papaya Salsa

1 pound dried apricots

1 small yellow onion, chopped

4 ounces golden raisins

1/2 cup red wine vinegar

1/4 cup blanched almonds, toasted

1 tablespoon freshly grated gingerroot

1 tablespoon minced garlic

1/2 teaspoon cayenne

salt to taste

1 small papaya, chopped

1 mango, chopped

1/4 cup red wine vinegar

Combine the apricots, onion, raisins and 1/2 cup vinegar with enough water to cover in a saucepan. Bring to a boil; reduce the heat. Simmer for 15 to 20 minutes or until of the consistency of honey, stirring occasionally. Do not overcook, as the mixture will thicken as it cools. Remove from heat.

Process the almonds, gingerroot, garlic, cayenne and salt in a food processor or blender until puréed. Stir into the apricot mixture. Add the papaya, mango and 1/4 cup vinegar and mix well. Chill, covered, for 2 hours or longer. Will keep for up to 3 weeks.

Yields 12 (1/2-cup) servings

David is another new host, having joined us in the summer of 1997. He graduated Cum Laude with a B.A. in Radio and Television and a minor in Advertising from Southern Illinois University at Carbondale. Dave always strives to "be good at what I do" and enjoys "relating to the viewers." His previous professional experience includes four years in the Marine Corps and doing sports radio in Chicago.

Tomato Bread

1 pound margarine, softened
2 teaspoons garlic powder, or
    16 cloves of garlic,
    minced
1 teaspoon pepper
2 teaspoons basil

2 teaspoons oregano
2 loaves French bread, cut
    into 1-inch slices
sliced tomatoes
sliced mozzarella cheese

Combine the margarine, garlic powder, pepper, basil and oregano in a bowl and mix well. Spread one side of each bread slice generously with the margarine mixture. Place in a shallow baking pan. Layer the tomatoes and cheese over each slice. Bake at 350 degrees for 15 to 19 minutes or until the cheese is melted.

    Yields 8 servings

DAVE SHIMKUS

107

Famous Baked Beans

4 slices bacon

1 (16-ounce) can pork and
beans

1$\frac{1}{2}$ tablespoons instant
minced onion

2 tablespoons molasses

2 tablespoons brown sugar

$\frac{1}{2}$ teaspoon MSG

2 drops of hot sauce

$\frac{1}{4}$ cup catsup

Cut one-half of the bacon into small pieces. Combine the pork
and beans, onion, molasses, brown sugar, MSG, hot sauce,
catsup and bacon pieces in a large bowl; mix well. Spoon into
a 1-quart baking dish. Arrange the remaining bacon over the
bean mixture. Bake at 375 degrees for 45 minutes or until the
bacon is cooked through and the bean mixture is hot and bubbly.

Yields 4 servings

The recipe for my baked

beans comes from my mom.

She is, for all intents and

purposes, the best cook in the

world. (Wolfgang Puck ain't

got nothin' on my mom.)

Tracey Edwards asked,

"Who says the baked beans

are famous? You can't just

say something is famous!"

"...Tracey Edwards...admitted that
they are the best baked beans she
has ever tasted."

Mexican Casserole

1 to 1½ pounds ground beef
1 to 1½ envelopes taco
    seasoning mix
12 small corn tortillas

1 (10-ounce) can enchilada
    sauce
1 to 2 onions, chopped
shredded Cheddar cheese

Prepare the ground beef with the taco seasoning mix using package directions. Dip the tortillas in the enchilada sauce in a shallow dish. Arrange 6 of the tortillas over the bottom of a 9x13-inch baking pan. Layer half the ground beef mixture, half the onions and half the cheese over the tortillas. Top with the remaining tortillas. Layer with the remaining ground beef mixture, onions and cheese. Pour the remaining enchilada sauce over the top. Bake, covered with foil, at 350 degrees for 40 minutes. Serve with chopped lettuce and chopped tomatoes.

Yields 10 servings

Low-Fat Substitutions: To reduce the fat grams, substitute ¾ pound ground turkey for the ground beef and replace half the cheese with fat-free Cheddar cheese.

For variety, add chopped bell pepper, pimento and/or cooked rice.

Well, whenever people came over to my parents' house for dinner, the first thing they would look for was baked beans. I have carried on this tradition with every party I throw. After attending one of my parties and partaking of the beans, Tracey Edwards swallowed her pride (and a lot of baked beans) and admitted that they are the best baked beans she has ever tasted.

Alan Skantz has sound experience as a newsman and also as an actor and a model before coming to The Home Shopping Network in 1991. Alan attended Arizona State University. He feels his most important job as a show host is "helping people understand what they're buying...and have fun doing it." He "fell in love" with helping our customers his first day on the job.

Stuffed Portobello Mushrooms

½ cup balsamic vinegar
¼ cup extra-virgin olive oil
½ teaspoon minced garlic
salt and pepper to taste
6 to 8 portobello mushrooms, stems removed
1 pound crab meat

1 (14-ounce) can artichoke hearts in water, quartered
½ cup cream cheese, softened
¼ cup mayonnaise
juice of 1 lemon
1 tablespoon Worcestershire sauce
4 plum tomatoes

Combine the balsamic vinegar, olive oil, garlic, salt and pepper in a bowl and mix well. Marinate the mushrooms in the vinegar mixture for 20 minutes. Combine the crab meat, artichoke hearts, cream cheese, mayonnaise, lemon juice, Worcestershire sauce, salt and pepper in a bowl and mix well. Remove the mushrooms from the marinade; discard the marinade. Grill the mushrooms over hot coals until they begin to get soft. Place them stem side up on a baking sheet. Cut each tomato into 5 slices and arrange on top of the mushrooms. Divide the crab meat mixture evenly and place firmly on top of the tomatoes. Bake at 350 degrees for 15 to 20 minutes or until the mushrooms are tender and the stuffing is heated through.

Yields 6 to 8 servings

ALAN SKANTZ

Happy Home Pot Roast and Veggies

1 (2½-pound) beef roast, slightly marbled
¼ teaspoon garlic powder
¼ teaspoon basil
¼ teaspoon parsley flakes
salt and pepper to taste
1½ tablespoons shortening
5 large potatoes or 8 to 10 red potatoes
½ package carrots, cut into quarters
mushrooms
onions, sliced

Sprinkle both sides of the beef with the garlic powder, basil, parsley flakes, salt and pepper. Brown both sides of the beef in the shortening in a Dutch oven over medium heat. Add just enough water to cover the roast. Bake, covered, at 350 degrees for 2 hours, adding additional water as needed to maintain the water level.

Add the potatoes and carrots to the Dutch oven. Bake for 45 minutes longer. Add the mushrooms, onions and any other vegetables desired. Bake for 15 minutes or until the onions are tender-crisp.

Yields 6 to 8 servings

Our family loves a good pot roast. My wife Cheryl is the queen of pot roasts, and here's what happens after a morning at church—we come home to the most beautiful aromas that help to make our happy home.

Alan Skantz

Pressure Cooker "Hot Legs"

10 medium chicken legs

1 (8-ounce) bottle barbecue
    sauce

¾ (12-ounce) bottle beer

Worcestershire sauce to taste

Tabasco sauce to taste

Heat a pressure cooker until hot. Add half the chicken. Cook for 1 minute or until brown on both sides. Add the remaining chicken. Cook for 1 minute longer or until brown. Add the barbecue sauce, beer, Worcestershire sauce and Tabasco sauce and mix well. Add the lid and seal. Cook over medium-high heat for 10 to 12 minutes or until the chicken is cooked through following pressure cooker manufacturer's instructions.

Yields 5 servings

"...I...made cooking history that night."

What do you do when the barbecue breaks down, company is on the way, and you promised some of the greatest barbecued chicken?

My first thought was to run to the nearest deli, grab some already-made barbecued chicken, and call it a night cooking. Nope. I remembered that we have a pressure cooker. It was time to put up or shut up, so I grabbed the cooker and made cooking history that night.

Perry has been with The Home

Shopping Network since the

beginning of 1998. He came to

us from a consumer electronics

company, where he served as

a regional training manager.

He is very detail-oriented

and outgoing, and his goal

here at The Home Shopping

Network is to give our

customers the most

information possible about

electronics,

so they can make a better

purchasing decision.

Tortilla Roll-Ups

8 ounces cream cheese, softened

1 cup sour cream

1 cup shredded sharp Cheddar cheese

1 (4-ounce) can chopped green chiles, drained

1 (4-ounce) can chopped black olives

1 to 2 tablespoons chopped onion

6 flour tortillas

Combine the cream cheese, sour cream, Cheddar cheese, chiles, olives and onion in a bowl and mix well. Spread the cream cheese mixture over the flour tortillas. Roll as for a pinwheel. Refrigerate, covered, for 1 hour. Cut into $\frac{1}{2}$-inch slices.

Yields 36 servings

PERRY SLATER

Party Potatoes

1 (32-ounce) package frozen
    hash brown potatoes,
    thawed
1 (10-ounce) can cream of
    chicken soup
2 cups sour cream
2 cups shredded sharp
    Cheddar cheese

$\frac{1}{2}$ cup melted butter
$\frac{1}{2}$ cup grated Parmesan cheese
1 teaspoon onion salt, or
    1 small onion, minced
1 teaspoon salt
$\frac{1}{2}$ teaspoon pepper
2 cups crushed cornflakes
$\frac{1}{4}$ cup melted butter

Combine the hash brown potatoes, soup, sour cream, Cheddar cheese, $\frac{1}{2}$ cup butter, Parmesan cheese, onion salt, salt and pepper in a bowl and mix gently. Spoon into a greased 9x13-inch baking dish. Toss the cornflakes and $\frac{1}{4}$ cup butter in a bowl. Sprinkle over the top of the potato mixture. Bake at 350 degrees for 40 to 45 minutes or until brown and bubbly.

    Yields 12 servings

My wife Nancy and I

are very outgoing people.

That was one of the many

qualities that made me

fall in love with her years

ago. We love to entertain,

especially in a casual

atmosphere with friends

and family.

"Enjoying one another is what
life is all about."

Perry Slater

Fudge Cake

1 teaspoon baking soda

½ cup buttermilk

2 cups sugar

2 cups flour

⅛ teaspoon salt

1 cup water

½ cup butter

½ cup shortening

2 ounces unsweetened chocolate

2 eggs

1 teaspoon vanilla extract

Chocolate Pecan Icing

Dissolve the baking soda in the buttermilk in a bowl. Mix the sugar, flour and salt in a bowl. Combine the water, butter, shortening and chocolate in a saucepan. Bring to a boil, stirring occasionally. Remove from heat. Add the sugar mixture and beat until smooth. Stir in the eggs. Add the buttermilk mixture and vanilla and mix well. Spoon the batter into a greased and floured 9x13-inch cake pan. Bake at 375 degrees for 30 to 35 minutes or until the cake tests done. Spread the Chocolate Pecan Icing over the warm cake.

Yields 15 servings

Chocolate Pecan Icing

½ cup butter

2 ounces unsweetened chocolate

6 tablespoons milk

1 (1-pound) package confectioners' sugar

½ cup chopped pecans

Combine the butter, chocolate and milk in a saucepan. Bring to a boil, stirring frequently. Remove from heat. Let stand until cool. Add the confectioners' sugar and mix well. Stir in the pecans.

The recipes we selected for this cookbook reflect our passion to have fun and live life to its fullest. These are simple recipes that are easy to prepare, taste great, the kids will love, and most of all, will free up more time for you and loved ones to spend quality time together.

Shannon first came to The Home Shopping Network in 1996 and was with us for a year at that time. She returned in April of 1998. Her previous work experience includes working for eight years as the Director of Feature Programming for an award-winning state radio network. She wrote, hosted, and developed entertainment programming syndicated in over 40 markets. The highlights of her career include attending the last five Academy Awards shows and producing a series of live broadcasts from Bosnia.

Pat's Best-Ever Carrots

1 pound carrots	grated peel of 1 orange
¼ cup packed brown sugar	1 (8¼-ounce) can crushed
3 tablespoons butter	pineapple, drained

Cut the carrots into strips. Cook in a small amount of water in a saucepan until tender-crisp. Combine the brown sugar, butter, orange peel and pineapple in a skillet. Bring to a boil. Add the carrots, stirring until glazed.

Yields 4 cups

SHANNON SMITH

Fruit Dip

Okay, so this fruit dip recipe is not for the "dieting crowd," but it sure is good!

8 ounces cream cheese, softened

1 (7-ounce) jar marshmallow creme

fresh fruit (apples, bananas, strawberries, pineapple)

Beat the cream cheese and marshmallow creme in a mixer bowl until blended. Chill, covered, until serving time. Serve with assorted fresh fruit. May spoon a small amount of caramel ice cream topping or strawberry jam in the center of the dip just before serving for a different twist.

Yields 2 cups

Some of my fondest images of family and friends back in Minnesota have taken place around the dining room table.

Shannon Smith

Oatmeal Cookies to "Write Home About"

2 cups flour

1 teaspoon baking soda

$\frac{1}{2}$ teaspoon salt

1 cup shortening

1 cup packed brown sugar

1 cup sugar

2 eggs

$\frac{1}{2}$ to 1 teaspoon vanilla extract

$\frac{1}{2}$ teaspoon almond extract

2 cups rolled oats

Sift the flour, baking soda and salt together in a bowl. Combine the shortening, brown sugar and sugar in a mixer bowl. Beat until creamy, scraping the bowl occasionally. Add the eggs, vanilla and almond extract and mix well. Add the flour mixture, beating until smooth. Stir in the oats. Drop the dough by teaspoonfuls onto greased cookie sheets. Bake at 350 degrees for 12 minutes or until light brown. Cool on cookie sheets for 2 minutes. Remove to a wire rack to cool completely.

Yields 4 dozen cookies

Even today, most of my quality time with family takes place around a home-cooked meal. I still miss the favorites that Mom and Grandma Lenore used to make. There's something incredibly inviting about those familiar delectable sensations and how food can transport you to another time.

Kathy Wolf has been at The Home Shopping Network since 1994. She has a degree in psychology from Southern Methodist University and also has studied at world-famous Oxford University in England. Her interesting career has included being chief financial officer for a yacht sales company. She says she really loves being with people— and it shows. Her people personality has led her to do charitable work for children with disabilities. And now she shares her love of life with our customers.

Mandarin Orange Salad

¼ cup vegetable oil

2 tablespoons sugar

2 tablespoons vinegar

1 tablespoon parsley

½ teaspoon salt

⅛ teaspoon pepper

⅛ teaspoon Tabasco sauce

¼ cup slivered almonds

1 tablespoon sugar

¼ head of lettuce

¼ head of romaine lettuce

2 ribs celery, chopped

2 green onions, chopped

1 (11-ounce) can mandarin oranges, drained

Combine the vegetable oil, 2 tablespoons sugar, vinegar, parsley, salt, pepper and Tabasco sauce in a small bowl and mix well. Sauté the slivered almonds in 1 tablespoon sugar in a skillet until the almonds are glazed. Combine the lettuce, romaine lettuce, celery, green onions, sugared almonds and mandarin oranges in a large bowl. Pour the vinegar mixture over the lettuce mixture. Toss gently.

Yields 6 to 8 servings

KATHY WOLF

Chicken Potpie

2 tablespoons butter
2 tablespoons flour
1 teaspoon salt
$\frac{1}{8}$ teaspoon (scant) thyme
$\frac{1}{8}$ teaspoon pepper
1 (15-ounce) can white
    chicken chunks, drained

1 (16-ounce) package frozen
    mixed vegetables, thawed
$\frac{1}{2}$ cup chicken broth
$\frac{1}{2}$ cup half-and-half
$\frac{1}{2}$ (10-ounce) can cream of
    mushroom soup (optional)
1 unbaked (10-inch) deep-dish
    pie shell

Heat the butter in a saucepan until melted. Stir in the flour, salt, thyme and pepper. Cook over low heat until thickened, stirring constantly. Add the chicken, mixed vegetables, broth, half-and-half and soup and mix well. Bring to a boil, stirring occasionally. Remove from heat. Spoon the chicken mixture into the pie shell. Bake at 425 degrees for 25 minutes.

Yields 6 to 8 servings

Low-Fat Substitutions: Substitute reduced-fat chicken broth for the chicken broth and nondairy fat-free creamer for the half-and-half.

Going to Nanny's house was always a treat as we knew the greatest of goodies was in store for us, and there was never a shortage. But the summer was always the best as there is nothing better than a light-tasting but ever-so-satisfying pie.

Kathy Wolf

Best-Ever Chocolate Chip Cookies

1½ cups sifted flour

1 teaspoon baking soda

1 teaspoon cinnamon

1 cup butter, softened

1 cup sugar

½ cup packed light brown
   sugar

1 egg

1 teaspoon vanilla extract

1½ cups old-fashioned
   rolled oats

1 cup semisweet chocolate
   chips

Mix the flour, baking soda and cinnamon in a bowl. Combine the butter, sugar and brown sugar in a mixer bowl. Beat until smooth, scraping the bowl occasionally. Add the egg and vanilla, beating well. Add the flour mixture and beat until blended. Fold in the oats and chocolate chips. Chill, covered with plastic wrap, for 1 hour. Shape the dough into 1-inch balls. Arrange 2 inches apart on greased cookie sheets; flatten slightly. Bake at 350 degrees for 10 to 12 minutes or until light brown around the edges. Cool on cookie sheets for 2 minutes. Remove to a wire rack to cool completely. May freeze the dough for future use, then defrost and make homemade cookies in minutes.

Yields 4 dozen cookies

Low-Fat Substitutions: To decrease the fat grams, substitute ¾ cup margarine for the butter and egg substitute for the egg.

125

CANDID KITCHENS

Our Outtake Favorites

Smoked Salmon Quesadillas

2 ounces mild goat cheese
1 tablespoon grated fresh
   horseradish or drained
   prepared horseradish
1 tablespoon sour cream
1 teaspoon chopped fresh
   dillweed
salt and freshly ground
   white pepper to taste

3 tablespoons extra-virgin
   olive oil
3 (7-inch) flour tortillas
4 ounces smoked salmon,
   cut into 6 thin slices
1 tablespoon chopped fresh
   dillweed
1 tablespoon fresh
   lemon juice

Combine the goat cheese, horseradish, sour cream, 1 teaspoon dillweed, salt and white pepper in a bowl and mix well. Heat the olive oil in a small skillet over medium-high heat for 1 minute. Fry the tortillas 1 at a time in the hot olive oil for 2 minutes or until light brown, turning once; drain.

Spread 2 generous teaspoons of the goat cheese mixture on each tortilla. Arrange 2 slices of the salmon on each tortilla. Sprinkle with 1 tablespoon dillweed and drizzle with the lemon juice. Cut each tortilla into 6 wedges. Serve immediately.

Yields 18 wedges

Our Outtake Favorite

Really Great Low-Fat Pizza

1 (4-ounce) can mushrooms

1 clove of garlic, minced

1 small onion, minced

¾ cup pizza sauce

1 (12-inch) pizza crust

½ (15-ounce) package low-fat ricotta cheese

1 (6-ounce) jar artichoke hearts

1½ cups low-fat mozzarella cheese

Sauté the mushrooms, garlic and onion in a nonstick skillet. Set aside. Spread the pizza sauce over the pizza crust. Layer with the ricotta cheese, mushroom mixture, artichoke hearts and mozzarella cheese. Bake at 350 degrees for 8 to 11 minutes or until the crust is golden brown.

Yields 4 servings

Veggie Squares

2 (8-count) cans crescent rolls

8 to 12 ounces cream cheese, softened

8 to 12 ounces salad-style mayonnaise

vegetables, such as broccoli, cauliflower, tomatoes, green onions

salt (optional)

Flatten and press together the crescent rolls on a baking sheet. Bake using package directions. Blend the cream cheese and mayonnaise in a bowl. Spread over the crescent roll crust. Chop finely the vegetables of choice and layer over the cream cheese mixture. Sprinkle with salt. Cut into 2-inch squares.

Yields 40 servings

Cheese Ball

16 ounces cream cheese,
softened

8 ounces spreadable
smoked Cheddar cheese

½ cup butter, softened

2 tablespoons milk

2 teaspoons steak sauce

chopped pecans

Beat the cream cheese, Cheddar cheese, butter, milk and steak sauce in a mixer bowl until fluffy, scraping the bowl occasionally. Chill slightly. Shape into a ball. Chill, covered, for 30 minutes. Roll in the pecans in a shallow dish. Chill, covered, until serving time. Serve with assorted party crackers.

Yields 12 servings

Fresh Salsa

4 red tomatoes, coarsely
chopped

1 Vidalia onion, minced

½ to 1 medium jalapeño or
to taste, minced

2 tablespoons minced fresh
cilantro

1 teaspoon salt, or to taste

Mix the tomatoes, onion, jalapeño, cilantro and salt in a bowl. Serve with tortilla chips, baked potatoes or omelets. Experiment with the amount of pepper, salt and cilantro and enjoy a spicy nonfat treat.

Yields 8 servings

Our Outtake Favorite

Soupe a la Crème d'Artichaut

6 large artichokes, stalks
   removed
4 quarts water
1 teaspoon lemon juice
3 cups milk
3 cups chicken stock
3 tablespoons butter
2 tablespoons flour

salt and freshly ground pepper
   to taste
2 tablespoons butter
1 cup chicken stock, boiling
¾ cup whipping cream, boiling
½ cup crushed hazelnuts,
   roasted
chopped fresh parsley to taste

Boil the artichokes in the water and lemon juice in a stockpot for
35 minutes or until tender. Drain upside down in a colander. Combine
the milk and 3 cups stock in a saucepan. Bring just to a boil. Melt
3 tablespoons butter in a heavy skillet. Stir in the flour. Cook over
low heat for 1 minute, stirring constantly. Add the hot milk mixture
gradually, whisking constantly. Add salt and pepper. Bring to a boil,
whisking constantly; reduce the heat. Cook for 1 hour, whisking
occasionally. Do not scorch! Scrape the edible pulp from the artichoke
leaves into a bowl; discard the leaves. Slice the artichoke bottoms to
remove the hearts; discard the bottoms. Chop the hearts. Braise the
pulp and hearts in 2 tablespoons butter in a covered skillet for
15 minutes. Season with salt and pepper. Purée the artichoke mixture
in a blender or food processor. Stir into the milk mixture. Strain
through a mesh sieve into a saucepan. Stir in 1 cup boiling stock
and boiling whipping cream. Cook just until heated through, stirring
frequently. Ladle into soup bowls. Top with the hazelnuts. Sprinkle
with parsley.

Yields 8 servings

Tex-Mex Cucumber Relish

2 unwaxed cucumbers

1 tomato, chopped

1 cup drained canned corn

1 green bell pepper, chopped

1 small red onion, chopped

5 tablespoons white vinegar

3 tablespoons sugar

1 tablespoon chopped
fresh cilantro

1 teaspoon red
pepper flakes

salt and freshly cracked
pepper to taste

Cut the cucumbers lengthwise into halves and thinly slice. Combine the cucumbers and next 4 ingredients in a bowl and mix gently. Add a mixture of the vinegar and remaining ingredients. Toss to coat. Chill, covered, in the refrigerator for up to 4 days.

Yields 6 to 8 servings

Jalapeño Wraps

16 ounces cream cheese,
softened

1 (10-count) package
flour tortillas

1 cup chopped jalapeños

Spread the cream cheese over the entire surface of the tortillas. Top with the jalapeños. Roll up the tortillas and cut into slices. Chill until serving time.

Yields 80 wraps

Pepper and Tomato Salad

2 banana peppers, coarsely
    chopped
2 tomatoes, coarsely chopped
1/2 teaspoon minced garlic

3/4 teaspoon basil
3/4 teaspoon salt
1/2 cup vegetable oil

Combine the banana peppers, tomatoes, garlic, basil and salt in a
bowl and mix gently. Add the oil and toss to coat. Chill, covered, in
the refrigerator until serving time.

    Yields 4 servings

Lime Pineapple Mold

1 (3-ounce) package lime
    gelatin
1 cup boiling water
8 ounces cream cheese, chilled
1 (8-ounce) can crushed
    pineapple, chilled

1 cup whipping cream,
    whipped
10 large maraschino cherries,
    chopped

Dissolve the gelatin in the boiling water in a bowl. Add the cream
cheese and mash with a fork. Stir in the undrained pineapple. Chill
until partially set, stirring occasionally. Fold in the whipped cream
and cherries. Spoon into an oiled mold. Chill, covered, until set.

    Yields 6 to 8 servings

Almond Punch

1 (12-ounce) can frozen
orange juice concentrate,
thawed

1 (6-ounce) can frozen
lemonade concentrate,
thawed

1 (46-ounce) can pineapple
juice

1 (12-ounce) can apricot nectar

$\frac{1}{2}$ cup (or more) sugar

$\frac{1}{2}$ to $\frac{3}{4}$ small bottle
almond extract

Prepare the orange juice and lemonade in a large container using package directions. Add pineapple juice, apricot nectar, sugar and almond extract and mix well. Chill until serving time. May freeze and serve slushy.

Yields 48 servings

June's Morning Soy Shake

1 cup calcium-enriched
soy milk

1 tablespoon powdered tofu,
or 1-inch cube fresh tofu

1 tablespoon honey

1 teaspoon vanilla extract

$\frac{1}{2}$ banana, or $\frac{1}{2}$ cup
strawberries or blueberries

6 to 8 ice cubes

Combine the soy milk, tofu, honey, vanilla, banana and ice cubes in a blender container. Process until smooth. May substitute 1 teaspoon light chocolate syrup for the fruit for a different flavor.

Yields 1 serving

Our Outtake Favorite

Aunt "Tonta" Ester's Potato Pancakes("Latkes")

6 large baking potatoes,
   peeled, shredded

2 large yellow onions,
   finely chopped

4 large eggs or equivalent
   amount of egg substitute

$^2/_3$ cup matzo meal flour or
   all-purpose flour

$^1/_2$ teaspoon salt

$^1/_2$ teaspoon pepper

3 cups vegetable oil

Rinse the potatoes in ice-cold water. Drain and press the potatoes to remove excess moisture. Combine the potatoes, onions, eggs, flour, salt and pepper in a bowl and mix well. Heat the oil in a deep skillet over medium-high heat. Spoon the batter into the hot oil with a large serving spoon, leaving a space between the pancakes. Cook until crisp and golden brown; do not overcook. Remove with a slotted spoon and drain on paper towels. Serve with applesauce or sour cream.

Yields 20 pancakes

Ratatouille

2 cups chopped eggplant

2 cups chopped zucchini

2 medium green bell peppers, chopped

2 medium tomatoes, chopped

2 cups chopped mushrooms

2 cups tomato juice

$1/4$ cup chopped fresh parsley

2 tablespoons minced onion

2 cloves of garlic, crushed

1 teaspoon oregano

1 teaspoon salt

1 chicken bouillon cube

shredded cheese

Combine the eggplant, zucchini, green bell peppers, tomatoes, mushrooms, tomato juice, parsley, onion, garlic, oregano, salt and bouillon cube in a stockpot and mix well. Bring to a boil; reduce heat. Simmer, covered, for 30 minutes or until the vegetables are tender, stirring occasionally. Remove the cover during the last part of the cooking process if the mixture contains too much liquid. Ladle into bowls. Sprinkle with cheese.

Yields 8 servings

Sweet Potato Supreme

3½ cups mashed cooked
   sweet potatoes

¾ cup sugar

¾ cup chopped black walnuts

⅓ cup milk

¼ cup melted butter or
   margarine

3 eggs, lightly beaten

1½ teaspoons vanilla extract

½ teaspoon salt

1 cup packed brown sugar

1 cup flaked coconut

½ cup chopped pecans

⅓ cup flour

3 tablespoons butter or
   margarine, softened

Combine the sweet potatoes, sugar, black walnuts, milk, melted butter, eggs, vanilla and salt in a bowl and mix well. Spoon into a lightly greased 2½-quart baking dish. Chill, covered, for up to 3 days. Mix the brown sugar, coconut, pecans, flour and softened butter in a bowl, stirring until crumbly. Chill, covered, for up to 3 days. Let the sweet potato mixture and brown sugar topping stand at room temperature for 30 minutes. Sprinkle the topping over the sweet potato mixture. Bake at 350 degrees for 40 to 45 minutes or until heated through.

Yields 8 servings

Big Onion Bread

3 tablespoons plus ½ cup margarine or butter

5 large onions, chopped

5 teaspoons salt

2 packages quick-rise yeast

8 ¾ cups (about) flour

2 cups milk

¼ cup light molasses

4 eggs

Melt 3 tablespoons margarine in a large skillet over medium-high heat. Add the onions and 1 teaspoon of the salt. Cook for 30 minutes or until tender and browned, stirring frequently. Remove from heat. Combine the yeast, 2 cups of the flour and the remaining salt in a large mixer bowl and mix well. Heat the milk, molasses and the remaining ½ cup margarine to 130 degrees in a saucepan. Beat the milk mixture gradually into the yeast mixture just until blended. Beat at medium speed for 2 minutes, scraping the bowl occasionally. Beat in 3 of the eggs. Beat in 3 cups of the flour. Beat for 2 minutes, scraping the bowl frequently. Reserve ⅓ cup of the onions. Stir in the remaining onions and 3½ cups of the flour. Knead the dough on a floured surface for 10 minutes or until smooth and elastic, working in the remaining ¼ cup flour. Place in a greased bowl, turning to coat the surface. Let rise, covered, in a warm place until doubled in bulk. Punch the dough down. Divide in half. Roll each half into a 15-inch rope. Twist the ropes together in a greased 10-inch tube pan; seal the ends. Bake at 350 degrees for 40 minutes. Beat the remaining egg in a cup with a fork. Brush the top of the loaf with the egg. Sprinkle with the reserved onions. Bake for 20 to 25 minutes or until golden brown. Cool in the pan for 10 minutes. Remove to a wire rack to cool completely.

Yields 20 servings

Brioche Mousseline

3 tablespoons lukewarm water	$\frac{1}{2}$ cup sugar
1 tablespoon dry yeast	1 teaspoon salt
1 teaspoon sugar	6 eggs
$3\frac{1}{2}$ cups flour	1 cup unsalted butter, softened

Combine the lukewarm water, yeast and 1 teaspoon sugar in a mixer bowl and mix well. Let stand in a warm place for 15 minutes. Mix the flour, $\frac{1}{2}$ cup sugar and salt in a bowl. Add very small amounts of the flour mixture alternately with the eggs to the yeast mixture, beating for 30 minutes or until a smooth dough forms. Add the butter 1 tablespoon at a time, beating constantly at high speed until blended. Let rise, covered, for several hours or overnight. Chill, covered, until ready to bake.

Brush three 1-pound coffee cans with melted butter and sprinkle with additional sugar. Divide the dough evenly between the prepared coffee cans. Let stand, covered with plastic wrap, until the dough has risen to the top. Bake at 400 degrees for 15 to 20 minutes. Invert onto a wire rack. Cool for 30 minutes. May bake in brioche molds.

Note: When making brioche with chilled dough, knead the dough lightly to warm it up. It will take longer to rise when the dough is cold.

Yields 36 servings

Our Outtake Favorite

Grandma Tilly's
Kasha Varnitchkes

1 top round beef

1 (13-ounce) package
    whole-grain kasha
    buckwheat groats

4 beef bouillon cubes

1 (16-ounce) package bow tie
    pasta

1 large onion, chopped

1 large package fresh
    mushrooms, sliced

butter

Place the beef in a slow cooker. Pour enough water over the beef to almost cover. Cook on Low until the beef falls apart. Prepare the kasha using package directions and adding the bouillon cubes. Cook the pasta using package directions; drain well. Sauté the onion and mushrooms in a small amount of butter in a skillet. Add the kasha, pasta, onion and mushrooms to the beef and mix well.

Yield is variable

Microwave Lasagna

1 pound ground beef

1 (32-ounce) jar spaghetti
  sauce

$\frac{1}{2}$ cup water

1$\frac{1}{2}$ cups ricotta cheese

1 egg, beaten

$\frac{1}{2}$ teaspoon salt

$\frac{1}{2}$ teaspoon pepper

8 uncooked lasagna noodles

8 ounces mozzarella cheese,
  shredded

2 medium eggplant, sliced

grated Parmesan cheese

Crumble the ground beef into a large glass bowl. Microwave on High for 2 to 3 minutes or until browned; drain. Stir in the spaghetti sauce and water. Combine the ricotta cheese, egg, salt and pepper in a bowl and mix well.

Spread one-third of the meat mixture over the bottom of a 9x13-inch baking dish. Layer the noodles, ricotta cheese mixture, mozzarella cheese, eggplant slices and remaining meat mixture one-half at a time over the meat mixture in the baking dish. Microwave on Medium, covered, for 8 minutes. Microwave on Medium, uncovered, for 30 minutes. Sprinkle with Parmesan cheese. Let stand, covered, for 15 minutes before serving.

Yields 6 to 8 servings

Our Outtake Favorites

Lasagna

2 pounds ground beef

8 ounces Italian sausage, crumbled

1 (16-ounce) can tomato paste

1 tablespoon parsley flakes

1 tablespoon basil

1 1/2 teaspoons salt

1 teaspoon sugar

1 teaspoon oregano

1 clove of garlic, minced

3 cups cream-style cottage cheese

1/2 cup grated Parmesan cheese

2 eggs, beaten

2 tablespoons parsley flakes

2 teaspoons salt

1/2 teaspoon pepper

8 ounces lasagna noodles, cooked, drained

16 ounces mozzarella cheese, sliced

Cook the ground beef and sausage in a skillet, stirring until brown and crumbly; drain. Stir in the tomato paste, 1 tablespoon parsley flakes, basil, 1 1/2 teaspoons salt, sugar, oregano and garlic. Simmer for 45 to 60 minutes or until of the desired consistency, stirring occasionally.

Combine the cottage cheese, Parmesan cheese, eggs, 2 tablespoons parsley flakes, 2 teaspoons salt and 1/2 teaspoon pepper in a bowl and mix well. Layer the noodles, cottage cheese mixture, mozzarella cheese and ground beef mixture 1/3 at a time in a baking pan. Bake at 375 degrees for 30 minutes. Let stand for 15 minutes before serving. May freeze for future use.

Yields 10 servings

Our Outtake Favorite

"Who Dat" in the Meat Loaf

1½ pounds ground beef

1 onion, chopped

1 green bell pepper, chopped

¼ cup milk

1 egg, lightly beaten

1 tablespoon Worcestershire
    sauce

¾ cup bread crumbs

1 teaspoon salt

½ teaspoon pepper

½ teaspoon garlic powder

kielbasa sausage

Combine the ground beef, onion, green bell pepper, milk, egg and Worcestershire sauce in a bowl and mix well. Add just enough of the bread crumbs to make the mixture adhere. Add the salt, pepper and garlic powder and mix well. Shape the mixture into a thick rectangle on a baking sheet lined with foil. Cut a large piece of the sausage and place in the middle of the rectangle. Fold over the edges of the foil to enclose the sausage.

Bake at 350 degrees for 45 to 55 minutes or until the ground beef and sausage are cooked through. May top with Cheddar cheese slices during the last few minutes of baking.

Yields 6 to 8 servings

Tater Tot Hot Dish

1 pound lean ground beef

$\frac{1}{2}$ cup rolled oats

$\frac{1}{2}$ cup milk

2 eggs, lightly beaten

$\frac{1}{4}$ to $\frac{1}{2}$ teaspoon red pepper
flakes (optional)

salt and black pepper to taste

1 (10-ounce) can cream of
chicken soup

1 (1-pound) package frozen
tater tots

Combine the ground beef, oats, milk, eggs, red pepper, salt and black pepper in a bowl and mix well. Spread over the bottom of a $2\frac{1}{2}$-quart baking dish. Pour the soup over the ground beef mixture. Arrange the tater tots over the top. Bake at 350 degrees for $1\frac{1}{4}$ hours.

Yields 8 servings

Western Brunch

12 slices of bread, buttered on
   both sides, crusts trimmed
3½ cups chopped ham
1 (6-ounce) can sliced
   mushrooms, drained
3 cups shredded Swiss cheese
4 eggs

2 cups milk
2 tablespoons mustard
1 teaspoon Beau Monde
   seasoning
dash of onion salt
1 teaspoon Worcestershire sauce
paprika

Layer the bread, ham, mushrooms, and cheese one-half at a time in
a greased 9x12-inch baking pan. Combine the eggs, milk, mustard,
Beau Monde seasoning, onion salt and Worcestershire sauce in a
blender container. Process until smooth. Pour over the layers. Sprinkle
with paprika.

Refrigerate, covered, for 8 to 12 hours. Bake at 325 degrees
for 1 hour. Let stand for 15 minutes.

Yields 12 servings

Stewed Chicken and Sausage

1 (3-pound) chicken, cut up
salt and freshly ground black
    pepper to taste
1/2 cup olive oil
6 hot or sweet Italian sausages,
    cut into thirds
4 cups julienned onions
2 cups chopped carrots
3 tablespoons chopped
    fresh garlic

1/2 teaspoon red pepper flakes,
    or to taste
2 cups chicken stock
2 cups dry white wine
2 cups tomato purée
2 tablespoons minced fresh
    rosemary
1/2 cup golden raisins

Season the chicken with salt and black pepper. Heat the olive oil in a Dutch oven or large saucepan over medium-high heat. Add the chicken. Cook for 3 to 4 minutes per side or until golden brown; drain. Remove the chicken and drain on a paper towel-lined plate. Add the sausages to the Dutch oven. Cook for 3 to 4 minutes or until browned, turning occasionally; drain well. Drain the sausages on a paper towel-lined plate. Combine the onions, carrots, garlic and red pepper flakes in the Dutch oven. Cook over medium heat for 5 minutes or until tender. Add the chicken stock, wine, tomato purée, rosemary and raisins; mix well. Add the chicken and sausages to the vegetable mixture, stirring to coat. Bring to a boil over high heat; reduce the heat. Simmer, covered, for 1 1/2 hours or until the chicken is cooked through and the sauce has thickened. Season with salt and black pepper.

Yields 6 servings

Our Outtake Favorite

Carol's Chicken Continental

1 (2-ounce) jar dried beef

6 slices bacon

6 medium boneless skinless
    chicken breast halves,
    poached

2 (10-ounce) cans cream of
    chicken soup

8 ounces cream cheese,
    softened

$1/2$ cup sour cream

garlic powder to taste

hot cooked rice

Line the bottom of a 9x13-inch baking pan with the dried beef. Arrange the bacon in a microwave-safe dish. Microwave until partially cooked; drain. Wrap 1 bacon slice around each chicken breast. Arrange the chicken in the prepared pan.

Combine the soup, cream cheese, sour cream and garlic powder in a saucepan. Cook over medium heat until heated through, stirring constantly. Pour over the chicken.

Bake at 350 degrees for 45 minutes or until light brown and bubbly. Serve over hot cooked rice with green peas and pearl onions.

Yields 6 servings

Pita Wedges

6 pita pockets

2 tablespoons olive oil

garlic powder to taste

oregano to taste

$1\frac{1}{2}$ cups fresh spinach

presliced mozzarella cheese

1 cup feta cheese

$1\frac{1}{2}$ cups chopped tomatoes

Place the pita pockets on a baking sheet. Brush each with olive oil. Sprinkle with garlic powder and oregano. Bake at 350 degrees for 8 minutes or until heated through and lightly browned. Combine the spinach with a small amount of water in a saucepan. Cook until tender; drain. Squeeze the moisture from the spinach. Layer the mozzarella cheese, spinach, feta cheese and tomatoes over the pita pockets. Bake until the mozzarella cheese melts.

Yields 36 servings

Chicken in Red Sauce

4 boneless skinless chicken
    breast halves
vegetable oil
1 medium onion, cut into
    halves, thinly sliced
1 (28-ounce) can whole tomatoes,
    drained, coarsely chopped

1 teaspoon ground cumin
1 large clove of garlic,
    crushed
chopped fresh cilantro
    to taste
salt to taste

Sauté the chicken in the oil in a skillet until brown on both sides; reduce the heat. Add the onion, tomatoes, cumin, garlic, cilantro and salt and mix well.

Simmer over low heat for 30 minutes or until the chicken is tender and cooked through, stirring occasionally. May add bread crumbs for a thicker consistency.

Yields 4 servings

Chicken and Dumplings

2 (10-ounce) cans cream of
    chicken soup

¼ cup water

1 teaspoon minced onion

½ teaspoon garlic salt

pepper to taste

3 boneless skinless chicken
    breasts, cut into
    bite-size pieces

1 (10-count) can buttermilk
    biscuits, cut into quarters

Combine the soup, water, onion, garlic salt and pepper in a large skillet and mix well. Stir in the chicken.

Cook over low heat for 2 hours or until the chicken is cooked through, stirring occasionally. Bring to a boil. Add the biscuits and mix well. Cook, covered, for 30 minutes, adding additional water as needed.

Yields 4 servings

Cherie's White Chicken Chili

1 large onion, minced

3 cloves of garlic, minced

¼ cup olive oil

1 (4-ounce) can minced
   green chiles

1 teaspoon chili powder

¼ teaspoon cumin

1 bay leaf

salt to taste

3 cups chicken broth

2½ pounds boneless skinless
   chicken breasts, cubed

2 (16-ounce) cans white
   cannellini beans,
   rinsed, drained

1 cup sour cream

salsa (optional)

shredded mozzarella cheese
   (optional)

shredded Cheddar cheese
   (optional)

chopped onion (optional)

Sauté the onion and garlic in the olive oil in a large saucepan for 10 to 12 minutes. Stir in the chiles, chili powder, cumin, bay leaf and salt; reduce the heat. Add the broth and chicken and mix well.

Bring to a simmer. Simmer for 15 to 20 minutes or until the chicken is cooked through, stirring occasionally. Stir in the beans. Cook over medium heat for 5 to 7 minutes; reduce the heat to low.

Discard the bay leaf. Add the sour cream, stirring just until blended. Ladle into chili bowls. Top each serving with salsa, mozzarella cheese, Cheddar cheese and/or chopped onion.

Yields 8 to 10 servings

Our Outtake Favorite

Cincinnati Chili

1 envelope chili seasoning mix

½ cup water

1 (15-ounce) can chopped
    tomatoes

1 pound soy meat or
    ground turkey

½ teaspoon baking cocoa

½ teaspoon cinnamon

1 (16-ounce) can red kidney
    beans, drained

8 ounces thin spaghetti,
    cooked al dente, drained

1 large onion, chopped

1 (8-ounce) package shredded
    sharp Cheddar cheese

1 (10-ounce) package oyster
    crackers

Combine the chili seasoning mix, water, tomatoes, soy meat, cocoa
and cinnamon in a large saucepan and mix well. Simmer for 1 to
1½ hours or until the flavors have blended, stirring occasionally.
Add the beans during the last 20 minutes of cooking.

Place the spaghetti on serving plates. Top each serving with
chili, onion, cheese and oyster crackers.

Note: It is not necessary to brown the meat before cooking
this chili. The chili has to be cooked longer but has a much richer
flavor. The kidney beans and oyster crackers may be omitted.

Yields 6 servings

Low-Fat Sicilian Stuffed Peppers

12 ounces turkey Italian sausage

1 cup fresh mushrooms

3 cups cooked brown rice

6 tablespoons grated nonfat or
   reduced-fat Parmesan
   cheese

6 large green bell peppers

2¼ cups marinara sauce or
   fat-free marinara sauce

¾ cup unsalted beef broth or
   vegetable broth

Brown the sausage in a large nonstick skillet sprayed with nonstick cooking spray, stirring until crumbly; drain well. Add the mushrooms. Cook for 2 minutes, stirring constantly and adding a small amount of water or broth if needed. Remove from heat. Stir in the rice. Add the cheese and mix well.

Cut the tops off the green bell peppers and remove the seeds and membranes. Spoon the sausage mixture into the peppers. Replace the tops.

Arrange the peppers upright in a 2½-quart casserole. Combine the marinara sauce and beef broth in a bowl and mix well. Spoon the sauce mixture around the peppers. Bake, covered with foil, at 350 degrees for 1 hour or until the peppers are tender.

Yields 6 servings

Our Outtake Favorite

Giblet Gravy

giblets and neck from a turkey

2 cups chicken broth

1 medium onion, chopped

1 cup chopped celery

$\frac{1}{2}$ teaspoon poultry seasoning

2 hard-cooked eggs, sliced

salt and pepper to taste

2 tablespoons flour

Cook the giblets and neck in the broth in a saucepan over medium heat until tender. Discard the neck. Chop the giblets. Return to the broth. Add the onion, celery and poultry seasoning to the broth. Cook over medium heat until onion and celery are tender. Stir in the egg slices, salt and pepper. Whisk the flour and a small amount of cold water in a small bowl. Stir into the broth mixture. Cook until of the desired consistency, stirring frequently.

Yields 2$\frac{1}{2}$ cups

Turkey Burgers

1 pound ground turkey

$\frac{1}{2}$ cup finely chopped onion

1 clove of garlic, minced

1 teaspoon seasoned salt

$\frac{1}{2}$ teaspoon Italian seasoning

$\frac{1}{2}$ teaspoon cumin

$\frac{1}{4}$ teaspoon thyme

$\frac{1}{4}$ teaspoon chili powder

$\frac{1}{8}$ teaspoon coarsely
    ground pepper

Combine all the ingredients in a bowl and mix well. Shape into 4 patties. Fry, broil or grill until the turkey is cooked through.

Yields 4 servings

Gucci Rolls

3 cups spaghetti sauce

1 (10-ounce) package frozen
    chopped spinach, thawed,
    drained

1 cup low-fat cottage cheese

$\frac{1}{4}$ cup minced onion

2 tablespoons grated Parmesan
    cheese

$\frac{1}{8}$ teaspoon pepper

$\frac{1}{8}$ teaspoon nutmeg

10 lasagna noodles, cooked,
    drained

nutmeg to taste

Spread a small amount of the spaghetti sauce over the bottom of a medium baking dish. Squeeze the excess moisture from the spinach. Combine the spinach, cottage cheese, onion, Parmesan cheese, pepper and $\frac{1}{8}$ teaspoon nutmeg in a bowl and mix well. Spread some of the spinach mixture down the center of each noodle. Roll to enclose the filling. Secure with a wooden pick.

Arrange the rolls in the prepared baking dish. Pour the remaining spaghetti sauce over the rolls. Sprinkle lightly with nutmeg to taste. Bake at 350 degrees for 25 to 30 minutes or until bubbly. Serve immediately.

Yields 10 servings

Our Outtake Favorite

Spicy Cajun Shrimp

1 cup butter

4 teaspoons crushed garlic

2 tablespoons olive oil

1/4 cup Worcestershire sauce

1/4 cup Tabasco sauce, or
to taste

lemon juice to taste

1 1/2 to 2 pounds unpeeled
shrimp

chopped fresh rosemary and
oregano to taste

8 ounces fettuccini or other
pasta, cooked, drained

Combine the butter, garlic, olive oil, Worcestershire sauce, Tabasco sauce and lemon juice in a saucepan. Cook for 5 minutes. Add the shrimp. Cook until the shrimp turn pink. Stir in the rosemary and oregano. Place the fettuccini on serving plates. Top with the shrimp mixture.

For added flavor, simmer the shrimp mixture for a while after the shrimp have turned pink.

Yields 6 servings

Pasta Vodka for Six

6 quarts water

21 ounces penne

6 tablespoons unsalted butter

1 cup less 1 tablespoon vodka

$1/2$ teaspoon red pepper flakes

1 cup (scant) canned Italian
    plum tomato purée

1 cup (scant) whipping cream

1 teaspoon coarse salt

1 cup grated Parmesan cheese

Bring the water to a boil in a large saucepan. Add pasta. Boil until al dente; drain. Cover to keep warm.

Heat the butter in a saucepan until melted. Stir in the vodka and red pepper flakes. Simmer for 2 minutes, stirring frequently. Stir in the tomato purée, whipping cream and salt.

Simmer for 5 minutes, stirring frequently. Toss with the warm pasta in a serving bowl. Sprinkle with the cheese.

Yields 6 servings

Our Outtake Favorite

Kentucky Whiskey Cake

1 pound red candied cherries

1½ cups chopped
   golden raisins

1 pint bourbon whiskey,
   brandy or rum

1½ cups butter, softened

2 cups sugar

1 cup packed brown sugar

6 egg yolks

5 cups flour

2 teaspoons nutmeg or
   cinnamon

1 teaspoon baking powder

6 egg whites, stiffly beaten

1 pound shelled pecans,
   lightly floured

Combine the cherries, raisins and whiskey in a bowl. Let stand for 8 to 12 hours. Cut patterns out of brown paper for the bottoms, sides and tops of a 10-inch and an 8-inch tube pan. Grease the pans and both sides of the paper. Line the bottoms and sides of the pans with the greased paper. Cream the butter, sugar and brown sugar in a bowl until smooth. Add the egg yolks 1 at a time, mixing well after each addition. Stir in the whiskey mixture. Sift the flour, nutmeg and baking powder together. Stir into the creamed mixture. Fold in the egg whites. Fold in the pecans. Pour into the prepared pans. Bake at 300 degrees for 30 minutes. Cover each pan with the greased brown paper tops. Reduce the temperature to 250 degrees. Bake the 8-inch cake for 3 hours and the 10-inch cake for 3½ hours. Serve chilled.

   Note: Cake can be made 1 week in advance to allow flavors to blend. Store in an airtight container with a bourbon-soaked cheesecloth placed in the center. Will keep indefinitely.

   Yields 42 slices

Strawberry Cake

3 cups flour

2¼ cups sugar

¾ teaspoon baking powder

1 teaspoon baking soda

½ teaspoon salt

1½ cups buttermilk

1 cup butter, softened

3 eggs

1½ teaspoons vanilla extract

3 (16-ounce) packages frozen
   strawberries, thawed,
   crushed

1 to 1½ cups sugar

Fluffy White Icing
   (see page 163)

Grease and flour three 9-inch cake pans. Line the bottoms with baking parchment. Combine the flour, 2¼ cups sugar, baking powder, baking soda and salt in a mixer bowl. Add the buttermilk, butter, eggs and vanilla. Beat until blended. Beat for 3 minutes longer, scraping the bowl frequently. Spoon the batter into the prepared pans.

Bake at 350 degrees for 35 minutes or until the layers test done. Cool in the pans for 15 minutes. Invert onto a wire rack to cool completely. Combine the undrained strawberries and 1 to 1½ cups sugar in a bowl and mix gently. Pierce the cake layers all over with a fork. Spoon the strawberries between the layers and over the top of the cake. Spread the Fluffy White Icing over the side and top of the cake.

Yields 20 servings

Our Outtake Favorite

Fluffy White Icing

3/4 cup sugar	1/8 teaspoon cream of tartar
1/4 cup water	2 egg whites, stiffly beaten
1 teaspoon corn syrup	1 teaspoon vanilla extract

Combine the sugar, water, corn syrup and cream of tartar in a saucepan and mix well. Boil over medium heat until a small drop dropped from a spoon spins a thread; do not stir. Pour the sugar mixture gradually over the egg whites in a mixer bowl, beating constantly. Beat until cool enough to spread. Stir in the vanilla.

Edna's Buttercream Icing

1 egg white	1 cup butter
1 cup sugar	1 teaspoon vanilla extract
1/2 cup milk, scalded	

Beat the egg white in a mixer bowl until stiff peaks form. Pour the sugar over the egg white. Drizzle with the milk. Cool for 15 to 20 minutes. Add the butter and vanilla. Beat until thick and creamy and of a spreading consistency, scraping the bowl occasionally.

Sour Cream Coffee Cake

1 cup shortening

1 cup sugar

4 eggs

1 teaspoon vanilla extract

1 cup sour cream

3 cups flour

$\frac{1}{2}$ teaspoon baking soda

1 tablespoon baking powder

Topping

Cream the shortening and sugar in a mixer bowl until smooth. Add the eggs and vanilla and mix well. Add the sour cream and blend thoroughly. Combine the flour, baking soda and baking powder in a bowl and mix well. Add the dry ingredients to the shortening mixture and mix well. Layer the batter and topping one-half at a time in a greased tube pan. Bake at 350 degrees for 45 minutes or until the cake tests done.

Yields 16 servings

Topping

$\frac{1}{2}$ cup chopped nuts

$\frac{1}{2}$ cup sugar

3 tablespoons flour

$\frac{1}{4}$ cup melted butter

1 teaspoon cinnamon

Combine the nuts, sugar, flour, butter and cinnamon in a small bowl and mix well.

Our Outtake Favorites

Mom's Cherry Squares

1 cup margarine, softened

1 cup sugar

1 teaspoon vanilla extract

2 eggs

2 cups flour

1/8 teaspoon salt

1 cup chopped walnuts

1 (21-ounce) can cherry
    pie filling

1/4 cup confectioners' sugar

Beat the margarine, sugar, vanilla and eggs in a mixer bowl until blended. Add the flour and salt and mix well. Stir in the walnuts. Spread 3/4 of the batter on an ungreased baking sheet with sides. Spread the cherry pie filling over the batter. Drop the remaining batter by spoonfuls over the pie filling. Bake at 350 degrees for 40 minutes. Let stand until cool. Sift the confectioners' sugar over the top. Cut into squares.

Yields 4 dozen squares

Chocolate Nut Bars

½ cup butter, softened

1 (2-layer) package yellow
    cake mix

2 cups flaked coconut

8 ounces semisweet chocolate
    chips or chopped
    semisweet chocolate

1 cup sugar

½ cup butter

¼ cup evaporated milk

3½ cups chopped pecans

Cut ½ cup softened butter into the cake mix in a bowl until crumbly.
Press over the bottom of an ungreased 10x15-inch baking pan.
Bake at 350 degrees for 20 minutes or just until the edges brown.
Sprinkle with the coconut and chocolate chips. Combine the sugar,
½ cup butter and evaporated milk in a saucepan. Bring to a boil.
Stir in the pecans. Pour over the baked layer. Bake for 25 minutes.
Cool on a wire rack. Cut into squares.

Yields 3 dozen

Colleen's Caramels

1 (14-ounce) can sweetened
   condensed milk
2 cups sugar
1 cup butter or margarine

1 cup corn syrup
1/2 cup chopped nuts (optional)
1 teaspoon vanilla extract

Combine the condensed milk, sugar, butter and corn syrup in a saucepan. Cook over medium heat until a candy thermometer registers 240 degrees, stirring constantly. Add the nuts and vanilla and mix well. Spread the mixture in a buttered 9x13-inch dish. Cut into 1-inch squares. Wrap each square in waxed paper. Store in a cool place. Do not allow the candy to cool too long before cutting.

Yields 72 pieces

Lisa's Rum Balls

1/4 cup instant coffee granules
1/4 cup rum
2 tablespoons baking cocoa
3 tablespoons corn syrup

1 cup confectioners' sugar
3/4 cup chopped walnuts
2 cups vanilla wafer crumbs

Dissolve the coffee granules in the rum in a bowl and mix well. Add the baking cocoa, corn syrup, confectioners' sugar, walnuts and vanilla wafer crumbs, mixing well after each addition. Chill, covered, for 2 hours. Shape into 1-inch balls and coat with additional confectioners' sugar. May use fat-free vanilla wafer crumbs for a lighter version.

Yields 36 rum balls

Our Outtake Favorites

Peanutty Cereal Bars

1 cup light corn syrup

1/2 cup packed brown sugar

1/4 cup sugar

1 cup peanut butter

6 cups cornflakes

1 cup coarsely chopped
   salted peanuts

1 (7-ounce) bar milk
   chocolate, melted

1/2 cup semisweet chocolate chips
   (optional)

1 teaspoon shortening (optional)

Line a 9x13-inch dish with foil. Grease the foil. Combine the corn syrup, brown sugar and sugar in a 3-quart saucepan. Bring to a boil over medium heat, stirring frequently.

Remove from heat. Stir in the peanut butter. Add the cornflakes and peanuts, stirring until coated. Pour into the prepared dish and press firmly. Spread with the melted milk chocolate.

Combine the chocolate chips and shortening in a saucepan. Heat just until melted, stirring frequently until blended and smooth. Drizzle over the top. Let stand until set. Cut into bars.

Yields 48 bars

Mom's Rice Pudding

1 quart milk

6 tablespoons sugar

5 tablespoons rice

2 eggs, lightly beaten

1 teaspoon vanilla extract

cinnamon to taste

Combine the milk, sugar and rice in a double boiler and mix well. Cook, covered, for 1 hour or until the rice is tender, stirring frequently. Stir $\frac{1}{4}$ of the hot milk mixture into the eggs in a bowl. Stir the egg mixture into the hot milk mixture. Cook over low heat until thickened, stirring frequently. Pour into a bowl. Stir in the vanilla and sprinkle with the cinnamon. Chill, covered, in the refrigerator until serving time. Recipe may be doubled.

Yields 4 to 6 servings

Our Outtake Favorite

Peach Tartlets

10 very ripe peaches, peeled,
  pitted, sliced, juice
  reserved

juice of 2 large limes or lemons

²⁄₃ cup (about) maple syrup

¹⁄₂ teaspoon cinnamon

pinch of freshly grated nutmeg

3 tablespoons instant tapioca

1 recipe (1-crust) pie pastry

Preheat the oven to 350 degrees. Combine the reserved peach juice, lime juice, syrup, cinnamon, nutmeg and tapioca in a large nonstick saucepan and mix well. Bring to a boil. Simmer, covered, for 10 minutes or until tapioca dissolves. Stir in the peaches. Cook for 2 minutes. Remove from the heat.

Roll the pie pastry into six 6-inch circles ¹⁄₈ inch thick on a lightly floured surface. Press each circle into a 4-inch tart pan that has been sprayed with nonstick cooking spray. Trim the edges even with the side of the pan. Spoon the peach filling into each tart, mounding ¹⁄₄ inch above the edge. Bake until tarts are set. Remove to a wire rack to cool.

Yields 6 tartlets

Pumpkin Bread

3 cups sugar

1 cup vegetable oil

4 eggs

1 (16-ounce) can pumpkin

3½ cups flour

1 teaspoon baking powder

1 teaspoon nutmeg

2 teaspoons baking soda

2 teaspoons salt

1 teaspoon allspice

½ teaspoon ground cloves

1 teaspoon cinnamon

⅔ cup water

1 cup chocolate chips
   (optional)

½ cup chopped nuts (optional)

Combine the sugar, oil, eggs and pumpkin in a mixer bowl and mix well. Add the flour, baking powder, nutmeg, baking soda, salt, allspice, cloves and cinnamon. Add the water and blend thoroughly. Stir in the chocolate chips and nuts. Pour into 2 greased 5x9-inch loaf pans. Bake at 350 degrees for 45 to 60 minutes or until the loaves test done.

Yields 2 loaves

Our Outtake Favorites

Index

Accompaniments. *See also* Salsas
    Giblet Gravy, 157
    Tex-Mex Cucumber Relish, 132

Appetizers. *See also* Dips; Snacks;
        Spreads
    Jalapeño Wraps, 132
    Pita Wedges, 150
    Really Great Low-Fat Pizza, 129
    Smoked Salmon Quesadillas, 128
    Tomato Bread, 106
    Tortilla Roll-Ups, 114
    Veggie Squares, 129

Artichokes
    Murphy's Artichoke Dip, 92
    Really Great Low-Fat Pizza, 129
    Soupe a la Crème
        d'Artichaut, 131
    Stuffed Portobello
        Mushrooms, 110

Asparagus
    Herb-Roasted Vegetables, 82
    Stove-Top Eye-of-Round with
        Spring Vegetables, 14

Bananas
    Dan's Carrot and Banana
        Supreme, 44
    Fruit Dip, 120
    Fruit Pizza, 66

Beans
    Black Bean, Corn and Tomato
        Salad, 85
    Cajun Red Beans and Rice, 16
    Cherie's White Chicken
        Chili, 154
    Cincinnati Chili, 155
    Colleen's Mexican Lasagna, 73
    Cremeans' Classic Hot and Spicy
        Bean Dip, 41
    Cremeans' Red Hot Pepper Chili, 40

Famous Baked Beans, 108
White Chili, 72

Beef. *See also* Ground Beef
    Carol's Chicken Continental, 149
    Grandma Tilly's Kasha
        Varnitchkes, 141
    Happy Home Pot Roast and
        Veggies, 112
    Stove-Top Eye-of-Round with
        Spring Vegetables, 14

Beverages
    Almond Punch, 134
    June's Morning Soy Shake, 134

Blueberry
    Blueberry Buckle Dessert, 98
    Fruit Pizza, 66

Breads, Loaves
    Mom Ferrera's Zucchini Bread, 50
    Pumpkin Bread, 172

Breads, Yeast
    Aunt Margie's Famous Yeast
        Rolls, 49
    Big Onion Bread, 139
    Brioche Mousseline, 140

Broccoli
    Chicken Divan, 76
    Momma Emily's Chicken Soup with
        Matzo Balls, 57
    Veggie Squares, 129

Cabbage
    Chinese Coleslaw, 61
    Dan's Homemade Slaw, 45
    Vietnamese Chicken Salad, 26

Cakes
    Christmas Cake, 12
    Fudge Cake, 117

Grandma Aggie's Cannoli
    Cake, 86
Grandma Marge's Chocolate
    Cake, 89
Italian Cream Cake, 18
Kelly's Carrot Cake, 81
Kentucky Whiskey Cake, 161
Red Velvet Cake, 46
Ruthie's Pineapple Upside-Down
    Cake, 48
Strawberry Cake, 162

Candy
    Buckeyes, 21
    Buttermilk Fudge, 101
    Colleen's Caramels, 168
    Lisa's Rum Balls, 168

Carrots
    Chicken Vegetable Stir-Fry, 56
    Dan's Carrot and Banana
        Supreme, 44
    Happy Home Pot Roast and
        Veggies, 112
    Kelly's Carrot Cake, 81
    Momma Emily's Chicken Soup with
        Matzo Balls, 57
    Pat's Best-Ever Carrots, 118
    Stewed Chicken and
        Sausage, 148
    Stove-Top Eye-of-Round with
        Spring Vegetables, 14

Chicken
    Baked Fried Chicken, 36
    Carol's Chicken Continental, 149
    Cherie's White Chicken Chili, 154
    Chicken Alfredo, 38
    Chicken and Dumplings, 153
    Chicken Divan, 76
    Chicken Enchiladas, 32
    Chicken in Red Sauce, 152
    Chicken Paprikash Soup, 58
    Chicken Potpie, 124

Chicken Vegetable Stir-Fry, 56
Dan's Tropical Chicken, 42
Mindy's Chicken Raspberry
    Salad, 88
Momma Emily's Chicken Soup with
    Matzo Balls, 57
Pressure Cooker "Hot Legs," 113
Rush Hour Chicken, 78
Stewed Chicken and Sausage, 148
Vietnamese Chicken Salad, 26
White Chili, 72

Chili
    Cherie's White Chicken Chili, 154
    Cincinnati Chili, 155
    Cremeans' Red Hot Pepper Chili, 40
    White Chili, 72

Chocolate
    Best-Ever Chocolate Chip
        Cookies, 125
    Buckeyes, 21
    Chocolate Nut Bars, 166
    Chocolate Pecan Icing, 117
    Fudge Cake, 117
    German Chocolate Frosting, 89
    Grandma Aggie's Cannoli Cake, 86
    Grandma Marge's Chocolate
        Cake, 89
    Lisa's Rum Balls, 168
    Peanutty Cereal Bars, 169
    Pumpkin Bread, 172

Coffee Cakes
    Sour Cream Coffee Cake, 164

Cookies
    Best-Ever Chocolate Chip
        Cookies, 125
    Grandmother Childs' Sugar Tea
        Cakes, 24
    Oatmeal Cookies to "Write Home
        About," 121
    Potato Chip Cookies, 52

Cookies, Bar
    Chocolate Nut Bars, 166
    Mom's Cherry Squares, 165
    Peanutty Cereal Bars, 169

Corn
    Black Bean, Corn and Tomato
        Salad, 85
    Tex-Mex Cucumber Relish, 132

Corn Bread
    Mom's Corn Bread Dressing, 25

Crab Meat
    Stuffed Portobello Mushrooms, 110

Desserts. See also Cakes; Candy;
    Cookies; Pies; Puddings
    Blanche Pettiford's Peach
        Dessert, 97
    Blueberry Buckle Dessert, 98
    Dan's Carrot and Banana
        Supreme, 44
    Fruit Pizza, 66
    Grandma Rene's Homemade
        Baklava, 54
    Mrs. Toombs' Peach Cobbler, 94
    Trifle, 74

Dips. See also Salsas
    Cremeans' Classic Hot and Spicy
        Bean Dip, 41
    Fruit Dip, 120
    Murphy's Artichoke Dip, 92

Egg Dishes
    Western Brunch, 147

Eggplant
    Microwave Lasagna, 142
    Ratatouille, 137

Fish. See also Salmon
    Country Onion Tart, 10

Easy Lemon-Garlic Grouper, 80
Easy Southern-Fried Catfish, 53

Frostings/Icings
    Chocolate Pecan Icing, 117
    Cream Cheese Frosting, 81
    Edna's Buttercream Icing, 163
    Fluffy White Icing, 163
    German Chocolate Frosting, 89
    Nutty Cream Cheese Frosting, 20

Ground Beef
    Colleen's Mexican Lasagna, 73
    Cremeans' Red Hot Pepper Chili, 40
    Easy Layered Spaghetti, 64
    Lasagna, 144
    Meatballs and Spaghetti Sauce, 33
    Mexican Casserole, 109
    Microwave Lasagna, 142
    Sloppy Joes, 32
    String Pie, 90
    Tacos, 30
    Tater Tot Hot Dish, 146
    Uncle Moe's South Philly
        Meatballs, 93
    "Who Dat" in the Meat Loaf, 145

Ham
    Cajun Red Beans and Rice, 16
    Western Brunch, 147

Mangoes
    Apricot, Mango and Papaya
        Salsa, 105
    Mango-Basil Salsa, 17

Mushrooms
    Chicken Vegetable Stir-Fry, 56
    Grandma Tilly's Kasha
        Varnitchkes, 141
    Happy Home Pot Roast and
        Veggies, 112
    Low-Fat Sicilian Stuffed
        Peppers, 156

Index

Minnesota Wild Rice Soup, 69
Momma Emily's Chicken Soup with Matzo Balls, 57
Ratatouille, 137
Really Great Low-Fat Pizza, 129
Rush Hour Chicken, 78
Stuffed Portobello Mushrooms, 110
Western Brunch, 147

Pasta. See also Salads, Pasta
Baby Vegetables with Pasta, 102
Cincinnati Chili, 155
Cremeans Fettuccini Alfredo, 38
Easy Layered Spaghetti, 64
Grandma Tilly's Kasha Varnitchkes, 141
Gucci Rolls, 158
Lasagna, 144
Microwave Lasagna, 142
Pasta Vodka for Six, 160
Spicy Cajun Shrimp, 159
String Pie, 90

Peach
Blanche Pettiford's Peach Dessert, 97
Mrs. Toombs' Peach Cobbler, 94
Peach Tartlets, 171

Peanut Butter
Bobbi and Noelle's Designer Fluffer Nutter, 20
Buckeyes, 21
Peanutty Cereal Bars, 169

Pies
Daddy's Favorite Lemon Meringue Pie, 22
Peach Tartlets, 171

Pork. See also Ham; Sausage
Uncle Moe's South Philly Meatballs, 93

Potatoes
Aunt "Tonta" Ester's Potato Pancakes ("Latkes"), 136
Happy Home Pot Roast and Veggies, 112
Party Potatoes, 116
Stove-Top Eye-of-Round with Spring Vegetables, 14
Tater Tot Hot Dish, 146

Puddings
Bread Pudding, 29
Mom's Rice Pudding, 170

Pumpkin
Pumpkin Bread, 172

Rice
Cajun Red Beans and Rice, 16
Carol's Chicken Continental, 149
Chicken Vegetable Stir-Fry, 56
Dan's Tropical Chicken, 42
Low-Fat Sicilian Stuffed Peppers, 156
Minnesota Wild Rice Soup, 69
Mom's Rice Pudding, 170
Roasted Acorn Squash with Wild Rice Salad, 104

Salad Dressings
Lime and Cilantro Dressing, 85

Salads, Congealed
Lime Pineapple Mold, 133
Pretzel Salad, 100

Salads, Main Dish
Blanche Pettiford's Shrimp Orange Salad, 96
Mindy's Chicken Raspberry Salad, 88
Turkey Salad, 68
Vietnamese Chicken Salad, 26

Salads, Pasta
Greek Macaroni Salad, 62

Salads, Vegetable
Black Bean, Corn and Tomato Salad, 85
Chinese Coleslaw, 61
Dan's Homemade Slaw, 45
Mandarin Orange Salad, 122
Pepper and Tomato Salad, 133
Roasted Acorn Squash with Wild Rice Salad, 104

Salmon
Grilled Salmon on a Bed of Spinach, 84
Poached Salmon Steaks, 17
Smoked Salmon Quesadillas, 128

Salsas
Apricot, Mango and Papaya Salsa, 105
Fresh Salsa, 130
Mango-Basil Salsa, 17

Sauces
DeHart's Midway-Style Barbecue Sauce, 60
Fresh Herb Sauce, 102

Sausage
Lasagna, 144
Low-Fat Sicilian Stuffed Peppers, 156
Sausage Heros with Peppers and Onions, 34
Stewed Chicken and Sausage, 148
"Who Dat" in the Meat Loaf, 145

Shrimp
Blanche Pettiford's Shrimp Orange Salad, 96
Shrimp Alfredo, 38
Spicy Cajun Shrimp, 159

Side Dishes
    Aunt "Tonta" Ester's Potato
        Pancakes ("Latkes"), 136
    Country Onion Tart, 10
    Dan's Carrot and Banana
        Supreme, 44
    Mom's Corn Bread Dressing, 25
    Stuffed Portobello Mushrooms, 110

Snacks
    Bobbi and Noelle's Designer Fluffer
        Nutter, 20
    Christmas Crazy Crunch, 70

Soups. *See also* Chili
    Chicken Paprikash Soup, 58
    Minnesota Wild Rice Soup, 69
    Momma Emily's Chicken Soup
        with Matzo Balls, 57
    Soupe a la Crème d'Artichaut, 131

Soy
    Cincinnati Chili, 155
    June's Morning Soy
        Shake, 134

Spinach
    Grilled Salmon on a Bed of
        Spinach, 84
    Gucci Rolls, 158
    Pita Wedges, 150

Spreads
    Cheese Ball, 130

Squash. *See also* Zucchini
    Roasted Acorn Squash with Wild
        Rice Salad, 104

Strawberry
    Fruit Dip, 120
    Fruit Pizza, 66
    Pretzel Salad, 100
    Strawberry Cake, 162

Sweet Potatoes
    Herb-Roasted Vegetables, 82
    Sweet Potato Crunch, 21
    Sweet Potato Supreme, 138

Turkey
    Cajun Red Beans and Rice, 16
    Cincinnati Chili, 155
    Giblet Gravy, 157
    Low-Fat Sicilian Stuffed
        Peppers, 156
    Turkey Burgers, 157
    Turkey Salad, 68

Vegetables. *See also* Names of
        Vegetables; Salads,
        Vegetable
    Baby Vegetables with
        Pasta, 102
    Herb-Roasted Vegetables, 82
    Chicken Vegetable Stir-Fry, 56
    Country Onion Tart, 10
    Veggie Squares, 129

Zucchini
    Mom Ferrera's Zucchini
        Bread, 50
    Ratatouille, 137

Index